Meet Me Within My Heart (दिल ही दिल में मिल)

A collection of poems on Love and Life

Abhash Singh

BookLeaf Publishing
India | USA | UK

Made with ❤ on the BookLeaf Publishing Platform
www.bookleafpub.in
www.bookleafpub.com

Dedication

For Papa, Mummy; Paju and Savi,
the ones who fought to make my dreams come true
when even I did not believe in them anymore.

For Siddhi, my wife...who came into my life like a storm,
and calmed the fires within.

पापा, मम्मी, पाजू और सावी के नाम-
जो मेरे ख़्वाबों के लिए तब भी लड़ते रहे,
जब मैं ख़ुद उन पर यक़ीन खो चुका था।

और सिद्धि के लिए- मेरी अर्धांगिनी,
जो तूफ़ान की भाँति आई ज़िंदगी में मेरे,
और भीतर जलते शोलों को सुकून में तब्दील किया।

Preface

ज़िंदगी को जितना समझा है,
बस उतना ही बयान करना चाहता हूँ।
गर कोई भूल हो गई हो, तो माफ़ करना;
शायर तो नहीं हूँ,
महज़ एक मामूली सा इंसान हूँ।
जज़्बातों की अपार महिमा को
शब्दों की सीमित क्षमता में
पिरोने की कोशिश की है।

I have understood life only in fragments,
and I've tried to give voice to just those.
If I've faltered anywhere,
I ask for your forgiveness;
for I am no accomplished poet,
merely an ordinary soul,
trying to weave the vastness of emotions
into the limited thread of words.

This book carries not just my voice, but my two tongues- English and Hindi. Some of these poems were first written in Hindi; some, first in English.

But they do not exist in one and simply echo into the other. I have made a sincere attempt to not make them literal translations, and more like retellings. Like trying to capture the soul, the essence of the thought that I first wrote the original poem in.

Each language offered a different doorway into the same feeling. Some things ache softer in Hindi, others bloom bolder in English. Where one breathes rhythm, the other hums stillness.

Each version exists fully. Not as a shadow of the other, but as a sibling. You may choose to read both or just one. Either way, you will hear the same heart speaking- just in different music.

इस किताब में सिर्फ़ मेरी आवाज़ नहीं है- बल्कि मेरी दो ज़बानों की बात है: अंग्रेज़ी और हिंदी।
कुछ कविताएँ पहले हिंदी में लिखी गईं,और कुछ सबसे पहले अंग्रेज़ी में आईं। लेकिन ऐसा नहीं है कि एक में लिखा और फिर दूसरी में बस अनुवाद कर दिया।

मैंने कोशिश की है कि हर कविता, हर भाषा में अपनी तरह से दोबारा जन्म ले। जैसे किसी एहसास की रूह को पकड़कर, दो अलग तरीक़ों से कहने की कोशिश हो।

हर भाषा ने उस एक ही भावना तक पहुँचने का एक अलग रास्ता दिया। कुछ बातों का दर्द हिंदी में ज़्यादा मुलायम लगता है, तो कुछ

जज़्बात अंग्रेज़ी में थोड़े और खुलकर सामने आते हैं।
जहाँ एक में बहाव है, वहाँ दूसरी में एक ठहराव की शांति। हर वर्ज़न पूरा है- कोई किसी का साया नहीं। बल्कि जैसे दो जुड़वाँ हों- अलग, पर एक जैसे।

आप चाहें तो दोनों पढ़ सकते हैं, या सिर्फ़ एक भी। किसी भी रास्ते से जाएँ- दिल की आवाज़ वही मिलेगी,
बस लहजा थोड़ा अलग होगा।

Acknowledgements

This collection is, in many ways, a sum of everything and everyone that has ever moved me.

To the filmmakers, musicians, poets, and songwriters- thank you. Every film I've watched, every song I've played on loop, every lyric that stayed with me longer than it should have... they've all shaped how I feel, how I write, and how I try to make sense of this world. Art has a way of reaching into places even I didn't know existed, and I owe so much of my emotional vocabulary to the works I've loved and lived with.

To my teachers, from school all the way through college- thank you for opening up the world to me. You might not remember the exact things you said, but I do. A sentence, a way of thinking, or even just your kindness. It mattered. It still does.

But most importantly, this book is because of the people I've met. The ones who stayed, the ones who left, and the ones who passed by for just a moment but still left something behind. Friends, strangers, loved ones, people I've fought with, laughed with, cried for, and lost- you've all taught me something about being human. About feeling deeply and trying to make sense of it.

Thank you. For the lessons, the memories, and for helping me understand not just art, but life.

यह किताब सिर्फ़ मेरी लिखी हुई नहीं है।

यह उन तमाम एहसासों, मुलाक़ातों और यादों का नतीजा है जिन्होंने मुझे कभी रुलाया, कभी हँसाया और कई बार चुपचाप बदल दिया।

उन फ़िल्म निर्देशकों, संगीतकारों, कवियों और गीतकारों का शुक्रिया, जिनकी रचनाओं ने मेरे भीतर के भावों को आवाज़ दी। न जाने कितनी फ़िल्में, कितने गीत, कितनी पंक्तियाँ- जो उस वक़्त मेरे लिए महज़ मनोरंजन नहीं, बल्कि सहारा थीं। कुछ शब्दों ने समझाया, कुछ धुनों ने थामा। जो महसूस किया, अक्सर उन्हीं से सीखा।

स्कूल और कॉलेज के मेरे सभी शिक्षकों का भी दिल से आभार। शायद आपको याद न हो कि आपने क्या सिखाया, लेकिन मुझे बहुत कुछ याद है। सोचने का तरीका, सवाल पूछने की आज़ादी, और सबसे बढ़कर- मानवीय बने रहने की समझ। ये सब मैंने आपसे ही सीखा।

लेकिन इस किताब का असली हिस्सा वे लोग हैं जिनसे मैं ज़िंदगी में कहीं न कहीं मिला हूँ। कुछ जो साथ रहे, कुछ जो बिछड़ गए, और कुछ जो बस एक लम्हे के लिए मिले लेकिन कोई असर छोड़ गए।

दोस्त, अजनबी, अपने, अपने-से लगने वाले; आप सबने मुझे इंसान होने का मतलब सिखाया। प्यार, दूरी, माफ़ी, पछतावा- इन सबकी शक्ल आपके ज़रिए समझ आई।

इस किताब की हर कविता में कहीं न कहीं किसी की परछाईं है।

आप सबका शुक्रिया- सिर्फ़ कला नहीं, मुझे ज़िंदगी समझाने के लिए।

Two Souls

Two souls, two, yes,
Fire beneath, under duress;
Trying to hold, hold, behold!
Hold each other, 'Oh! So bold,'

Shout out the others, two;
Yes, two, two of them too.
Pulling the souls, apart, apart,
Pulling apart, part by part;

Fire beneath, burning so hot;
Hot and scorching; scorching hot.

The pull, strong; the fire, pain,
Pain, Pain, Pain but no gain;
No gain, none, nothing at all,
Love, love, love; downfall,

Fall, fall, fall down, yes;
Fall apart, an unsorted mess,

The pull, the fire; all of them yes,
Yes, yes, under duress,
Two souls, only two; yes.

दो रूह

दो रूह थीं, हाँ बस दो,
दिल में धुआँ, और नीचे लौ।

रोकें, थामें, थमे हुए,
इक-दूजे में मानो जमे हुए।

बाक़ी चीख़ें - 'क्यूँ ये साथ?'
हाँ, वो भी दो ही थे जनाब !

खींचें उनको, करें अलग,
हर चीख में दर्द रहा था सुलग।

नीचे शोला, दहकती ज़मीं,
दिल में अंगार पर साँसों में नमी।

खींच बहुत थी, जलन बेहिसाब ,
दर्द, दर्द, दर्द का सैलाब।

ना हासिल कुछ, ना कोई जीत,
मोहब्बत की यही तो है रीत।

गिरते पढ़ते टूटते दिन रात,
बिखरा प्यार, अधूरे जज़्बात।

वो खिंचाव, वो शोला, वही सज़ा है याद,
बेतुकी सी तन्हा वफ़ा की फ़रियाद।

दो रूह थीं, हाँ बस दो,
दिल में धुआँ, और नीचे लौ।

दिल ही दिल में मिल

दिल ही दिल में मिल
पर मिल तो जा सही
तू ख्वाब में तो आ,
गर नज़र में ना सही।

हर ज़र्रे में तो अब,
सिर्फ तेरी ही छवि,
ये क्या है हो गया?
क्या तुम ही हो वही?

के दिल ही दिल में मिल,
पर मिल तो जा सही,
तू ख़्वाब में तो आ,
ग़र नज़र में ना सही।

ग़र मिल भी हो रही
गर हो भी जो वही,
तो क्या करूं सही?
ख्याल लेके बस,
फिरूं मैं हर कहीं।

के क्या ही है ग़लत,
और क्या ही है सही
तू रूबरू तो आ,
और फिर बता यूं ही।

के दिल ही दिल में मिल,
पर मिल तो जा सही,
तू रूह तो दिखा,
ग़र जिस्म ना सही।

के दिल ही दिल में मिल,
पर मिल तो जा सही
गर ख्वाब में नहीं,
तो खयाल ही सही
गर गुफ्तगू नहीं,
तो इल्तज़ा सही।

Meet me within my heart

Meet me, even if just within my heart,
But do so... don't break me apart.
Come to me like a midnight's dream,
If not in the warm sun's gleam.

In every beginning, in every truth,
In every corner, every nook;
What magic's come to be?
Is it you I truly see?

So meet me, if just within my heart
But meet me, don't break me apart.
Come to me like a midnight's dream,
If not in the warm sun's gleam.

And if we meet, *if* we do
If that soul is truly you,
Then tell me, what even is true?
I drift with just a name,
A thought... a flickering flame.

What's wrong, and what feels right?
Step forth, step into light.

And let me tell you, true and free,
What in the world you mean to me.

So meet me, if just within my heart,
Meet me... don't break me apart.
Peer into my soul, let me be your spark,
And in this heart of mine, leave your mark.

Yes, meet me, if just in heart
But meet me, play your part.

If not in dream's embrace,
Then thought shall take its place.

If not in whispered speech,
Then let my humble prayer reach.

I Can't Breathe

I CAN'T BREATHE,

But you don't care;
No, not anymore, or do you?
I want to believe,
Because you seem to.
But you seem to for all the things,
That I don't need you to, right now.
You care about tomorrow,
But what about tomorrow?
If I can't make it today- because,
It burns when I inhale,
It pierces when I exhale;
It pains from limb to limb,
Like an existence gone stale.

I CAN'T BREATHE,

Is that bothering you still?
Are you irritated yet? Annoyed?

Have you had enough of a fill?
Or do you want more of the quiet?
The quiet you think is solace,
But how would you know?
Have you ever been in a place,
Which rains hellfire and snow?

I CAN'T BREATHE,

'What's wrong?' You ask
Can't you see?
My lungs won't swallow,
And fingers can't form a fist,
My heart won't slow down,
Do you want a full list?
Well, won't be able to
Make that for you too.
Pretence, you might think,
And all I wish
Was that you were right.
Would love for this to be an act,
And not my being on the brink.

I CAN'T BREATHE,

The air's getting heavy,
But my heart; heavier.

I feel a little dizzy,
So let me slump down,
Into a cocoon,
Of my madness and despair,
While you look at this mess,
Thinking what all to repair.

I CAN'T BREATHE,

But let it be now,
I don't think you shall
Ever comprehend this.
Because you say,
'Everything's fine, ain't it?'

I CAN'T BREATHE...

But I guess it'll pass.
Because that's what
You say as well.
I look for support,
But I find pity,
Is that the death knell?

I CAN'T BREATHE...

But you can.

And I envy you,

Because I can't.

साँस नहीं ले पा रहा हूँ

साँस नहीं ले पा रहा हूँ...
पर तुम्हें फ़र्क़ पढ़ता है क्या?
या शायद बिल्कुल ही नहीं
गर मान लूँ की तुम मान रही हो
क्या सच में ये क्या है जान रही हो?

तुम सोचो कल की सुबहों को,
मैं आज की साँसों में जलता हूँ।
कह दो ना, कैसे जियूं मैं,
जब हर पल भीतर से गलता हूँ।

साँस नहीं ले पा रहा हूँ,
तुम्हें अब भी कोफ़्त सी होती है?
या बस ये चुप्पी भाती है?
तुम मानो इसे सुकून भरा,
पर ये चुप्पी तो चीख़ों से सजी हुई रातें हैं।
कभी जली हो क्या ऐसी आग में,
जहाँ बर्फ़ भी तपती हो साथ में?
जहाँ साँसें छाले छोड़ती हों,
और घुटन सी हो हर बात में?

साँस नहीं ले पा रहा हूँ,
"क्या हुआ?" तुम पूछती जाती हो,
पर क्या नज़रें कुछ कहती नहीं?
फेफड़े जैसे पत्थर बन बैठे,
धड़कन भी अब रुकती नहीं।
उँगलियाँ कांपें, मुट्ठी न बनें,
लफ्ज़ हों पर जुबां ना चलें।

साँस नहीं ले पा रहा हूँ,
कैसे बताऊँ तुम्हें लफ़्ज़ों में?
जो हाल मुझे ख़ुद बेहाल कर रहा है,
शब्दों में कैसे सजाऊँ उन्हें?
तुम सोचो मैं बस नाटक करता,
काश! वही होता तो अच्छा होता।
काश! ये सब एक किरदार होता,
और मैं बस झूठा सच्चा होता।

साँस नहीं ले पा रहा हूँ,
हवा है भारी, दिल और भारी,
दुनिया लगे अधूरी सारी।
बैठ जाने दो मुझे वहीं,
जहाँ मेरा दर्द बसा रहता है।
जहाँ दीवारें कुछ कहती हैं,
और छत से भी पानी बरसता है।
तुम सोचो क्या जोड़ा जाए,
पर हर हिस्सा यहाँ बिखरता है।

साँस नहीं ले पा रहा हूँ,
अब छोड़ो बात समझने की,
कह दो ना के सब ठीक है फिर से,
गर झूठा ही हो मगर
दिलासा शायद पल भर का सुकून दे जाये।

साँस नहीं ले पा रहा हूँ...
शायद ये भी गुज़र ही जाएगा,
तुम भी तो यही कहती रहती हो।
मैं ढूंढूं काँधा, पर नसीब आए दया,
क्या यही है आख़िरी सजा?

साँस नहीं ले पा रहा हूँ...
पर **तुम** ले पाती हो,
और मैं जलता हूँ तुमसे
क्योंकि **मैं नहीं।**

मुक़द्दर

मुक़द्दर से बग़ावत करने हम चले थे,
शिद्दत हमारी अधूरी थी;
राह में आगे हँसकर वो चली,
क्यूँकि चाहत की ना मंज़ूरी थी।

किसी ओर चली थी वो,
किसी ओर चले थे हम;
बढ़ती गई दूरी थी।
मुक़द्दर से बग़ावत करने हम चले थे,
शिद्दत हमारी अधूरी थी।

साँसें हम ले रहे थे,
धड़कनें भी कहीं सुनाई देती थी;
ज़िंदा होने का एहसास तो था,
मगर आँखों में ये सपने,
पल रहीं कई अधूरी थीं;
मुक़द्दर से बग़ावत करने हम चले थे,
शिद्दत हमारी अधूरी थी।

अब भटके किसी पथिक की तरह,

बस राह पर ये पाँव हैं चल रहे;
पर शिकायत इनसे भी क्या करूँ,
रूह ही तो हमारी जल रही थी,

आहटों की आस लगाए बैठा;
उस कमबख़्त की भी तो ये मजबूरी थी,
आख़िर हम तो मुक़द्दर से लड़ बैठे,
जिस कारण शिद्दत कल भी अधूरी थी,
शिद्दत कल भी अधूरी होगी।

Fate

We tried to defy fate,
But love… ours; was never whole.
She smiled and walked ahead alone,
Because my name wasn't on her soul.

She chose a path I couldn't take,
And I walked mine, heart half-awake.
The space between just grew and grew;
The truth of us, only silence knew..

We tried to defy fate,
But our fire came too late.

I breathed, I moved, I spoke, I stayed,
But something deep inside had frayed.
Yes, I was alive, so to speak;
But dreams inside had grown too weak.
They bloomed and withered in my eyes,
Like quiet veracities dressed up as lies.

We tried to defy fate,
But destiny stood at the gate.

Now I wander, like the lost ones do,
Feet still moving, but no clear view.
And how can I blame the road or rain,
When it's my soul that holds the pain?

Still waiting for a voice, a sign,
But maybe her silence was also mine.
We fought a war we couldn't win...
And that's where endings must begin.

We tried to defy fate,
But maybe we were too late.
Because we tried to defy fate,
But our destinies stood steadfast at the gate.

बात

बात सबसे करता हूं,
पर बात किसी से होती नहीं है;
ये कैसी सी तन्हाई है,
जो भीड़ में भी खोती नहीं है।

ये कैसी अजीब अनबन है,
अंधेरी रातों को भी सोती नहीं है;
ये कैसी बेरुखी हंसी है,
खुशी की मुस्कान पिरोती नहीं है।

आंसू भी गर टपक जाये
ग़म महसूस होती नहीं है;
शक्ल गीली तो हो जाती है,
पर रूह को वो भीगोती नहीं है।

सपने भी धुंधला से गए हैं,
मन को कोई चुनौति नहीं है;
बात सबसे होती है मेरी;
पर बात किसी से होती नहीं है।

I Speak To All, Yet Speak To None

I speak to all, yet speak to none,
Lonely in a crowd, I come undone.

What strange and silent void is this?
That lingers on, unknown, unmissed?

A quarrel dwells beneath my skin,
Even darkest nights can't tuck it in.
What cold and hollow laugh I wear,
It holds no joy, just vacant air.

The tears may fall; my cheeks may wet,
But sorrow hasn't landed yet.
My face is soaked in quiet grief,
But not a drop brings soul relief.

The dreams have blurred, their colors pale,
My heart no longer lifts its sail.
I speak, I smile, I nod, I run...

But truth be told, *I speak to none.*

The One Who Could Never Be Your Mystery (A memoir in seven parts)

ONE

On a dusky street of no repute,
Where neon lights did softly mute
The clamour of lives in passing glare;
I met you once. You sat right there.

A random café, a corner seat,
With coloured glass fogged by the heat
Of tired souls and steamy brews,
And lonely hearts in paper shoes.

Your eyes were not just eyes you see
They held a hush, a secrecy.
As if behind their silent gleam,
Dwelt fragments of a deeper dream.

A hundred faces passed me by,
All clothed in laughter, veiled in sigh,
But yours alone refused to fade,
A page the universe hadn't made.

And I, adrift on currents strange,
Felt something in my orbit change.
The world fell still, as time withdrew,
And all that moved... *it moved through you.*

TWO

Oh, what a chase I made of you!
A tempest dressed in morning dew.
Not love, perhaps, not yet defined;
But something fierce, a feeling unrefined.
A hunger not for skin or bone,
But for your *you*, for you alone.

Each breath you drew, I wished to hold,
Like whispered prayers; too deep, too bold.
Each smile of yours lit fires within,
Each touch sent sparks all over my skin.
I called it love, for so they said;
The poets, songs, the books I read.

And hence I spoke; I told you all.
The earth stood still, but did not fall.
No violins, no thunderclap...
Just traffic's sigh and tires' slap.
You said "I love you" back to me,
And all I felt was... *apathy*.

No triumph flared within my chest,
No storm, no quake, no fiery crest.
Just blinking lights and crowded air,
A hundred faces everywhere.

THREE

We dated then, as couples do;
The café now; a table for two.
We shared our days, our cups, our words,
Like matching socks in drawers of thirds.

But something lacked; some wild delight,
Some madness blooming in the night.
The quiet yawn of distant stars
So close, yet so far...

I searched your eyes; your gaze was kind,
Yet in that gaze, my own decline.

I watched myself, from far away,
Becoming him who would not stay.

The river stretched, grew cold, grew wide.
I on this bank, and you that side.
Each step you took to meet my shore
Was met by mine, two back, then evermore.

You saw, you knew, but dared not ask.
The questions wore a lover's mask.
And so I broke it; left you bare.
I left, though part of me stayed there.

FOUR

What silence fell upon my days!
A fog too thick, a thoughtless haze.
The world grew dim, its colours dry;
Each morning felt like asking why.
You'd filled some part I didn't name,
And when you left, I stayed the same,
But hollower, like half a line
That's sung without its second rhyme.

So one fine day, I turned around.
I traced your steps, I sought that sound.

I walked again that careless street,
Where strangers cross and rarely meet.
And there you were… my void undone,
A borrowed light, a rising sun.

You smiled. You laughed. You raised your brow.
And all my pain dissolved somehow.

FIVE

But wait! What was this thing I felt?
Not love, not grief, not joy that dwelt
In fairytales or tearful plays,
Not passion's spark nor longing's haze.
It was an echo, not a flame,
A truth too soft to have a name.

Perhaps I never loved at all.
Perhaps I built too high a wall
Of dreams I learned from here and there,
From people afraid to lay themselves bare.

You see, to name a thing is wrong,
To call a feeling weak or strong.
To box it in with brittle speech
Is to condemn what lies out of reach.

For what is "love"? Just four short sounds;
Too slight to hold where soul unbounds.

What I had felt for you, my dear,
Was neither clean nor crystal-clear.
It was a warmth, a pulse, a breath,
Not something owned by life or death.

SIX

But when I named you “mine,” you see,
The world began to whisper to me;
Its clauses, codes, its “shoulds” and “musts,”
Its faithful bonds and sacred trusts.
We lived not love, but what it meant,
With rules and roles already spent.

I wanted more, or maybe less.
I longed for love that didn’t press.
You sought the whole, and I... the part.
You gave your all, I gave my heart.
Not whole, but fractured, shifting, frail,
A boat too thin to brave a gale.

I held an ideal in my hand,

A castle built of sinking sand.
And so we sank, and so we broke,
On truths no one ever spoke.

SEVEN

But still, you are my mystery;
A page I read unknowingly.
Not for the plot, not for the twist,
But for the fact that it exists.

To see you once, just once, today...
In some café along the way,
To pass you like a fleeting tune
Beneath the amber hush of noon;
Is all I ask, is all I'll need.
A life unbound by want or greed.

I do not wish to own your name,
Nor burn once more in passion's flame.
I want to see you in the crowd,
And let my silence speak out loud.

I want to know you, but never know,
To hold, and yet to let you go.
To drift within your orbit wide,

And never once step to your side.

You are not love, nor memory;
You are the breath of mystery.

The sacred blur, the unread part,
The pulse beneath my aging heart.

And though I'll never call you "mine,"
In random days and streets and time,
You'll rise like ink in rainy skies;
A poem I write with just my eyes.

Yours faithfully,
The one who could never be your mystery.

वो आभास जो तुम्हारा एहसास ना बन सका
(हमारी कहानी, मेरी ज़ुबानी)

दिलकशी

किसी गुमनाम गली की शाम थी,
जहाँ रौशनी भी कुछ बदनाम थी,
सूरज की छाया कुछ मद्धम सी थी,
हर आवाज़ जैसे शोर की संगम सी थी।

वहीं एक कैफ़े की कोर में तुम,
रंगीन काँच के शोर में तुम।
गर्म कॉफ़ी की भाप में भीगी अधूरी बातें,
थकी रूहें, काँपती साँसें।

तुम्हारी आँखें बस आँखें न थीं,
मानो चुप्पियों की परछाईं थीं।
हर पल में कोई राज़ था गहरा, हर झलक में कोई ख्वाब सुनहरा

सौ चेहरे थे, हर एक पर नक़ाब,

हँसी थी झूठी, और आहें बेहिसाब।
पर तुम ठहर गई यूँ वक़्त की चाल में,
जैसे कायनात रुक सी गई हो सवाल में।

और मैं,
जो बहता था यूँ ही कहीं,
थम गया था उस पल, वहीं।
सब कुछ रुका, सब कुछ थमा,
बस तुम थीं... और दिल खुशनुमा।

ऊँस

तुमसे मिलने की जो लगन थी,
वो कोई मंज़िल नहीं, अगन थी।
ना नाम था, ना परिभाषा,
बस एक बेचैनी, एक तमाशा।
ना जिस्म की चाह, ना कोई वादा,
पर रूह का तुमसे था इरादा।

हर साँस जो तुमने ली,
लगती जैसे मेरी ही थी।
हर मुस्कान से मानो उठी चिंगारी,
हर स्पर्श बने पुकार हमारी।

कोई जुनून था, कोई लगाव,
शायद मोह, शायद भ्रमित भाव।
कहा सभी ने- “ये इश्क़ है”,
तो मैंने भी सोचा; शायद यही सच है।

और फिर, जो दिल में था, बोल डाला,
दिल को संदूक सा खोल डाला।

पर जब तुमने कहा की "हाँ इश्क़ है मुझे भी",
दिल बोला; "क्या बस इतना ही था?"
ना काँपती धरती, ना झुका आसमान,
बस सड़कों की आवाज़ और धुँआ-धुआँ जहान।
ना कोई संगीत, ना आँसू-भरे गीत,
ना बिजली, ना बारिश, ना मोहब्बत की रीत।

यही तो कहते आए थे शायर,
जब इश्क़ हो तो दुनिया भूल जाओगे,
और खुदकी छवि सिर्फ़ उनमें पाओगे...
फिर ना जाने क्यों वो हुआ नहीं,
क्या मेरी मोहब्बत ही झूठी थी?

इश्क़

फिर रोज़ वही मुलाक़ातें थीं,
वही बातें, वही मुस्कानें थीं।

कैफ़े वही था, मेज़ वही थी,
पर अब न कोई बात नई थी।

कपों में चाय भरी जाती थी,
पर दिल में कोई बात न आती थी।
हर दिन जो साथ बिताया हमने,
मानो जैसे धुँध में धुँदलाये सपने।

कुछ था जो पहले गुनगुनाता था,
अब हर साज़ एक समान था।
तुम पास थीं, पर दूर कहीं,
और मैं, खैर मैं तो था ही नहीं।

तुम्हारी आँखों में इक सवाल था,
जो अब भी होंठों पे ख़ामोश बेहाल था।
मैं जानता था, गर पूछ लेती तुम,
टूट के बिखर जाता ये जो भी था।

तो मैंने ही पहले तोड़ दिया,
वो रिश्ता जो हमने जोड़ा था।
पर जाते-जाते कुछ रह गया,
कुछ अब भी था तुम्हारे पास पड़ा।

अक़ीदत

तेरे जाने के बाद कुछ ख़ास न था,
हर लम्हा अधूरा, हर साँस थमा।
रंग थे, मगर उनमें चमक न रही,
सवेरा तो आया; पर दुपहरी नहीं।

हर सुबह उठता तो लगता यही,
कि दिन बस गुज़रने की रस्म सही।

तेरी जगह जो भरती थी हर बात में,
अब एक सन्नाटा था; हर आवाज़ में।

कभी बेवजह चल पड़ता था मैं,
तेरी गलियों से होकर फिर वहीँ।
जिस मोड़ पे तुझसे पहली बार मिला,
उसी मोड़ पे फिर तेरा चेहरा खिला।

और एक दिन, एक बार फिर वही,
वही कैफ़े, वही खिड़की, वही रोशनी।
तू बैठी थी फिर, उजास बनी,
तेरी हँसी की वो जानी पहचानी सी खिलखिलाहट।

तू मुस्काई, जैसे बरसों की धूप,
जैसे लौट आई हो एक पल में रूप।
और कुछ तो टूटा, कुछ जुड़ सा गया,
जो तन्हाई थी, वो कहीं उड़ सा गया।

इबादत

तुझसे मिलकर जो सुकून आया,
उसमें ना कोई शोर था, ना साया।
ना वो मोह, ना वो मोहब्बत की आग,
सिर्फ़ एक भरा दिल था; थोड़ा हल्का, थोड़ा ख़ास।

और तब पहली बार ये सोचा मैंने;
शायद कभी चाहा ही नहीं तुझे वैसे जिसको कहते हैं "इश्क़"।
शायद तू बस एक एहसास थी,
जो नाम दिए बिन भी बहुत पास थी।

ना तुझमें कोई कमी थी, ना मैं अधूरा था,
पर जो था हमारे बीच; शायद वो ना पूरा था।
जो दुनिया ने समझाया, वही मान लिया,
पर जो दिल ने जाना; उसकी ना कभी सुनी।

शब्दों के दायरे तंग बहुत हैं,
भावनाएँ उनसे कहीं बड़ी हैं।
"प्यार" कह देना, ज्यों जाल बिछाना,
और उस जज़्बे को छोटी परिभाषा में बाँध आना।

जो था मेरे भीतर, वो मौन था,
ना कोई दावा, ना प्रश्न, ना उत्तर।
बस एक गर्माहट थी... जैसे धूप हो,
जो जलाए नहीं; पर छू जाए हर कोर।

जुनून

पर जिस दिन तुझे "अपना" कहा,
वहीं से शायद रिश्ता डगमगाया था।

तेरे नाम पे जब मेरा हक़ बना,
उस दिन मोहब्बत पीछे छोड़ आया था।

दुनिया ने समझाया; अब ये करना,
अब ये निभाना, अब ऐसे चलना।
हम इश्क़ न रहे, इक फ़र्ज़ बन गए,
हर जज़्बा अब आदर्श बन गए।

तू चाहती थी सब कुछ मेरा,
मैं दे सका बस आधा सवेरा।

तू समंदर थी; बेहद, बिन किनारा,
मैं किनारा, जो डरता तेरी गहराई से सारा।
जिसे बारिश से डर था हर रोज़,
और तू वही बारिश थी- बेमौसम, बेहिसाब, बेज़ोर।

हम टूटे; पर कोई आवाज़ नहीं आई,
ना तकरार, ना विदाई, ना रुलाई।
बस एक मौन था जो पलकों पे ठहरा,
और वहीं से सब कुछ भीतर से बिखरा।

मौत

फिर भी...
तू रह गई मेरे लिए एक सवाल,
जिसका जवाब न ज़रूरी था, न बेमिसाल।
ना जानना था, ना भूलना तुझे,
बस हर रोज़ इक नज़र में ढूँढना तुझे।

किसी मोड़ पर, किसी भीड़ में कहीं,
तेरा दिख जाना; बस इतना ही सही।

ना पुकारना, ना कुछ कहना,
बस चुपचाप इक पल तुझमें बहना।

ना तू मेरी थी, ना मैं तेरा हुआ,
पर ये रिश्ता किसी लफ़्ज़ से परे हुआ ।

ना वादे, ना कसमें, ना दस्तूर,
फिर भी दिल ने माना के तू थी जरूर।

तेरे पास होकर भी पास न जाना,
तेरे इर्द-गिर्द रहकर भी दूर ही रहना।

तेरा होना ही मेरे लिए काफी है,
तेरी मुस्कान अब भी मेरी ताज़गी है।

तू इश्क़ नहीं, ना कोई अफ़साना,
तू बस वो एहसास है... जो समझ न आना।

एक अधूरी बात, जो पूरी न हो,
पर अधूरी रहकर भी सबसे खूबसूरत हो।

सप्रेम,
वो आभास जो तुम्हारा एहसास ना बन सका।

The Letter She Asked For

Write you a letter, you say?
Of things that make me fall for you?
Or describe your eyes in the most eloquent form?
But what else shall I say today?
Or what shall I differently do?

Or in what way shall I let my thoughts perform?
This dance of rhymes and fancy words,
That you ask me to today showcase;
Are like mindless little flapping birds,
That shall fly away, the first chance they get.

Words, so hollow so empty,
Their existence dependent;
On usage aplenty.
How can hollow vessels ever contain in its entirety,
The profoundness of an emotion so vast?
Isn't the connection of souls more treasured?
Or was it just a thing of the past?

I do not find the need to write you a letter in ink,
Because I feel I write one everyday,
When you are in my heart, with every breath and blink;
What's the need of a paper anyway?

We are one, and that togetherness prevails,
There's a connection that none can explain,
There's a warmth that none can cool,
There's a peace that none can attain;
There's a life that none can have,
There's a doubt none can ascertain,
There's a touch of something magical,
There's something that can defeat pain.

With so many things already in place,
What's to say and what's to hear?
You asked for a letter from me today,
But what's there that you don't already know, my dear?
What's there that you don't already know my dear;
When for you, my soul has always been bare?

ख़त

तुम कहती हो के एक ख़त लिखूँ।
उन बातों का ज़िक्र जो तुम्हें फिर से मोहब्बत का एहसास दिला दे ;

या तुम्हारी आँखों को किसी ऐसे शब्द में ढालूं,
जो खुद भी तुम्हारे आगे झुक जाएं?
मगर अब और नया क्या कहूं तुमसे?
कौन सा ज़रिया चुनूं जो पहले न किया हो कभी?
किस कला से फिर ये ख़्याल सजाऊं?
किस ढंग से उन्हें आज उकेरूं?

जब सारे ख़याल ही इतने तेज़ हों...
उड़ जाती हैं... ओझल... पकड़ में न आएं।
फिर क्या है महत्व... बेटुकी इन बातों का...

क्या ये लफ़्ज़; जो बड़े भारी हैं,
पर अंदर से कुछ खाली हैं
उनसे संतुष्टि होगी तुम्हें?
काफ़ी होंगे तुम्हारे लिए?
अगर हो भी जाएं...
तो मुझे नामंज़ूर है।

क्या ये खोखले शब्द समेट पाएंगे,
वो जज़्बात जो नज़र भी बयान न कर सके?
स्याही से क्यों दर्ज करूं वो बात,
जब हर सांस तुम्हारा नाम दोहराती है?

जब हर पल तुम ज़हन में बसी हो मेरे
तो काग़ज़ की ज़रूरत ही क्या रह जाती है?
जब दिल ही रोज़ तुम्हारा ख़त बन जाए,
हर धड़कन तुम्हारे नाम की मिसाल हो,
तो हाथ से लिखा एक खत; उसकी कोई औक़ात है क्या?

हम एक हैं- ये कहने की ज़रूरत नहीं रही।
बस समझ में आए सो ज़रूरी
एक राहत है जो किसी तूफ़ान से भी न दबे।
एक ठण्डक है जो भीड़ में भी खामोश कर जाये।
एक एहसास है जो शब्दों की मोहताज नहीं।
कुछ ऐसा है जो हर दर्द को परास्त कर दे।

जब इतना सब पहले से है,
तो और क्या ही क़हदूँ तुमसे आज?
तुमने मुझसे एक ख़त मांगा था,
पर क्या कुछ ऐसा है जो तुम जानती नहीं?

क्या कुछ ऐसा है जो रह गया अब तक अनकहा,
जब मेरी रूह हर रोज़ तुम्हारे नाम की कविता रचती है?

The Lake That Called Itself A Dream

A mile or two from my broken gate,
A lake once sighed beneath its weight.
Not loud. Just low, in whispered threads,
Where Papa walked with heavy treads.

Its name was strange; a bitter word,
"Ambition," though no bird had stirred
its waters smooth as shattered glass,
its surface still as futures passed.

He'd gaze; not forward, but within,
His eyes would flicker, then begin
to glisten not from wind or sun,
but something old, undone, *undone.*

He said,
"Had I once braved that trembling blue,
perhaps my dreams would have flowered too."
His voice would drag like rust on stone;

and I would nod.
But not alone.

For I too dreamt. I too could feel
those waves that curled like fate's own seal.
My chest held fire, my steps held rage;
a bird too young to know its cage.

And so
one dusk, without a word,
no final thought, no sound was heard,
I leapt into that breathless blue
to chase what Papa never knew.

But now the light begins to fade.
The sky dissolves in deeper shade.
The far shore doesn't drift in near.
It isn't far...
*it **isn't** here...*

Have I been fooled by names they gave?
Was this a lake
or just a grave?

I swam, I swam, I kicked, I cried
but dreams don't bloom on the other side.
The name, oh the name! It played its trick:

they called it "lake,"
but it runs deep.

Too deep.
Too wide.
Too dark.
Too quick.

Now breath is thread,
my arms are smoke,
each wave a hand around my throat.
I want to rest, not die, not sleep;
but rhythm drags me through the deep.

If someone hears... if someone dares...
tell Papa not to chase what's there.
For what lies "there"
was never real.

No light. No edge.
No ground to feel.

Tell him, soft
so he won't weep:
the lake he feared
is far less steep
than this one,

where I swam too far;
in search of dreams
that drown like stars.

स्वप्न झील

मेरे आशियाँ से कुछ मील दूर,
एक प्यारी सी झील हुआ करती थी;
जिसके तट के समीप अक्सर,
पापा और मैं टहला करते थे ।

बड़ा अजीब नाम था झील का,
हर कोई उसे "महत्वकांशा" कहता था ।

उसे देखकर पापा की आँखों में,
एक अजीब सी चमक आजाती थी;
मानो जैसे उन लहरों की आवाज़,
उन्हें धीरे धीरे तड़पाती थी ।

अफ़सोस में अक्सर कहते मुझसे,
"उस पार ज़िंदगी ख़ुशहाल होगी कितनी ।
काश उस पार तैरने की हिम्मत की होती,
तो आज शायद सपने पूरे हो चुके होते।"

ये बात चुभ जाती थी दिल को,
अमाँ मियाँ सपने तो कई हम भी देखते थे !

दिल में अरमा हमारे भी थे कई,
पूरा करने का जज़्बा भी रखते थे ।

इस डर से की कहीं,
बुढ़ापे में हमें भी अफ़सोस ना हो;
एक दिन चुपचाप कूद पड़े हम झील में,
ये सोचकर की उस पार पोहोंच,
ज़िंदगी को खुलकर जिएँगे ।

कई पहर हो गए अब तो,
किनारा क्यूँ नहीं मिल रहा आख़िर?

कहीं हमें टोपी तो नहीं पहना दी लोगों ने,
समंदर को झील बुलाकर?

थकान सी महसूस हो रही है,

साँस फ़ूल रही है अब;

घुटन सा लग रहा है,

क्या मैं डूब रहा हूँ?

शायद सर चकरा रहा है,
ज़रा आराम करना चाहता हूँ;

पर करूँ कैसे?

लहरों की तेज़ रफ़्तार ने,
रुकना नामुमकिन सा कर दिया है ।

अगर कोई सुन रहा है,
ज़रा जाकर कहना ना मेरे पापा से;
की अफ़सोस ना करें उस पार होकर,
क्यूँकि इस पार तो कोई पार ही नहीं है ।

NOTHING

I asked for nothing
and nothing answered.
Not the sky,
not flame,
not the calm of sleep,
just a slow collapse
into something deeper than deep.

I had hoped to feel.
Even pain would do.
But the dark,
it doesn't bleed.
It swallows you.

No stars, no fire, no funeral hymn
just silence pressing bone to skin.

"You called," it said,
not loud, but vast

like church bells ringing
through a sea of glass.

"You begged for rest,"
the voice intoned,
"and so my dear,
I brought you home."

A pause.
A breath.
But I had none.

"Where is this?" I asked.
The dark just hummed.

"I thought death would feel,"
I said, ashamed.
"I thought I'd cry,
or burst in flame!
Or find some peace!
Or laugh like a madman!"

The voice replied:
"This is your fate.

You wanted out,
you got your wish.

This is the void.
An empty dish."

It came to me then,
the shape I wore.
A shadow dressed
in mere metaphor.

"Who are you?" I said aloud.
It laughed and bowed;
not cruel, not proud,
just calm,
like water in a ruined pool.

"I'm the god you drew in charcoal breath,
when you played at life
but longed for death."

"You think I'm cruel,
but I'm precise.
I gave you time,
I gave you dice.
You rolled for silence.
You chose the end.
Now here we are,
my only friend."

"I had nothing to live for!" I cried in vain.
"No joy, no home, just nameless pain."

It shook its head.
"You had the fire.
You just forgot
you could aspire."

"What of those
who smiled your way?
Who stayed
when you pushed them away?

What of the books
you left unread?
The girl
who wept beside your bed?

What of the days
you cursed and spent;
but never asked
where living went?"

I closed my eyes,
but even there,
the weight of light

was hard to bear.

“You are me,” it said,
“and I am you…
The part that hoped,
the part that knew.

You wore me once
like second skin;
then sold me off
to rot within.”

“Why now?” I asked,
“Why even speak?”
“Because you finally
felt the weak.

You felt the void,
its bitter kiss.
And now you know
what nothing is.”

“I want to live,” I whispered slow,
though shame had nowhere else to go.
“I want the mess,
the ache, the dawn.
I want to feel

where I belong."

The god just smiled,
a crooked grace.
"You've seen the dark.
Now earn your place."

A gasp.
A pull.
A distant light.
The taste of blood.
The curse of sight.

My body: wrecked,
but somehow whole.
A war between
the flesh and soul.

The beeping sang.
The wires danced.
And I
was given
one more chance.

So if you see me,
know I've been
to places past

where men have sinned.

And if I smile,
it's not from glee
but knowing what
I failed to see:

That death is quiet,
cold, and long.
But life,
however cracked,
is *song*.

ख़ालीपन

मैंने मांगा ख़ालीपन
और मिला मौत का आलिंगन।

ना कोई रौशनी, ना साया,
ना कोई सपना, ना ही माया।

ना आसमान ने पुकारा,
ना किसी काँधे का सहारा।
ना नींद ने आँचल फैलाया,
बस एक गहरी खाई में,
गिरता रहा,
बेआवाज़, बेगराज।

मैंने चाहा था कुछ महसूस हो जाए,
दर्द ही सही; पर कुछ तो पाएँ।
मगर घोर काली स्याही सा अँधेरा,
वो बहाता नहीं,
वो बस निगलता है, और लौटाता नहीं।
ना तारे, ना चिता का गीत,

बस सन्नाटा जो सूनेपन से भी भीत।

“तुमने बुलाया,”
किसी ने कहा,
आवाज़ जैसे टूटी शीशियों का नशा।
“छुटकारा माँगा था न,
तो लो, ये रहा तुम्हारा ठिकाना।”
एक विराम।
एक साँस।
पर साँस भी अब कहाँ बची थी पास।
“ये कहाँ है?” मैंने पूछा
जवाबी सन्नाटे से अँधेरा भी गूँज उठा।

“ लगा था मौत कुछ और होगी,”
शर्म से बोला मैं,
“एक चीख़, एक अलाव,
या कोई राहत; कोई संग चलती हवा।
मगर यहाँ तो... कुछ भी नहीं है!”

वो बोला;
“यही है वो इनाम
जो तुमने मांगा था
एक सन्नाटे का बंजर जाम।”

फिर एक साया आया; हुबहू मुझसा ही,
बस थोड़ा धुंधला, थोड़ा कमज़ोर, थोड़ा अधूरा।

"तुम कौन हो?" मैंने पूछा
वो मुस्कराया, झुका, और कहा
"मैं वो हूँ
जिसे तुमने रच लिया था,
कभी ख़ुदा समझकर,
और कभी ख़ुद को मिटा कर।"

"मैं बेरहम नहीं,"
उसने कहा,
"मैं वही वक़्त हूँ
जिसे तुमने सूली चढ़ाया।
मैं वो रास्ता हूँ
जिसे तुमने मुड़कर देखा भी नहीं,
वो आवाज़
जिसे तुमने सुनकर भी अनसुना छोड़ दिया।"

"तुम कहते हो
जीने के लिए कुछ था ही नहीं?"
तो फिर वो लोग
जो बिना कहे साथ थे कहीं?
वो मुस्कानें जो तुम्हारी ख़ामोशी में भी ठहरी रहीं,
वो हाथ जो तुम्हारे छूटते वक़्त भी थमे नहीं?
वो किताबें जो तुम्हारी धड़कनों की तरह बंद रहीं,
वो लड़की जो सिरहाने पास रोती रही?"

मैंने आँखें बंद कीं,

पर रौशनी का बोझ अब भी आँखों पर चढ़ा रहा।

"तुम मैं हो,"
उसने कहा,
"और मैं वो हिस्सा
जिसे तुमने खुद से अलग माना।
मैं उम्मीद हूँ; जो कभी जलती थी,
वो अरमान; जो कभी पलकों में पलती थी।

तुमने मुझे पहना था; कभी ज़िद की तरह,
फिर उतार फेंका; किसी बेक़द्र सज़ा की तरह।"

"अब?" मैंने पूछा,
"अब क्यों?"
उसने कहा:
"क्योंकि अब तुम सच मान गए हो,
और क्या होती है मौत जान गए हो।
अब तुम जान चुके हो
'ख़ालीपन' कैसा लगता है।
कैसा होता है
वो शून्य, जो ज़िन्दगी की जगह लेता है।"

"मैं जीना चाहता हूँ,"
मैंने धीरे से कहा,
"बिखर के, लड़ के, थक के सही
पर जीना चाहता हूँ।"

"मुझे फिर से वो अधूरी साँसें चाहिए,
वो नासमझी, वो कड़वाहट, वो सुबह की चाय।
मुझे जीना है
क्योंकि अब मरना भी कुछ नहीं दे पाए।"

वो मुस्कराया
जैसे मित्र हो पुराना
जिसे शायद कभी समझा ही नहीं था।
"तो चलो," उसने कहा,
"अब अपनी जगह कमाओ;
और जिसे दर्द और शिकस्त माना,
उसे पूजा की तरह अपनाओ।"

एक साँस खींची मैंने,
एक खिंचाव आया,
कहीं से फिर रौशनी लौटी।
जैसे अंधेरे ने हार मान ली हो।

खून का स्वाद,
आँखों में तेज़ सफेदी;
और कहीं, किसी कोने में
एक धड़कन की गूँज।

मशीनों की आवाज़ें
फिर से धड़कती थीं।
और मैं
एक अधूरे वादे की तरह,

जी उठा।

अगर अब मुझे मुस्कराते देखो,
तो समझ लेना,
मैं वहाँ से लौटा हूँ
जहाँ मौत भी थककर बैठ जाती है।
और अगर मेरी मुस्कान
थोड़ी बोझिल लगे
बुरा ना मान ना
अब मैं जानता हूँ
कि *ख़ालीपन*
दरअसल किस क़दर भरा हुआ होता है।

यादों की कश्ती

ये यादों की कश्ती,
ये सपनों का पानी;
छुपी इनमें है,
कहीं मेरी कहानी।

इस दरिया के दिल में,
दफन वो कहीं है;
उतर के भी ढूँढा,
नहीं है, नहीं है।

ये मेरी कहानी,
मेरी ज़िंदगानी;
वो यादों की कश्ती
वो सपनों का पानी;
दफन ही रहे,
तो हो मेहरबानी।।

The Boat Of Dreams

The boat of dreams,
memory in streams.

It drifts alone
through flesh and bone.

My tale lies deep,
where waters sleep,
buried in silt,
in hush, in guilt.

I dove, I bled;
No trail, no thread.
No voice replied,
No past survived.

This life I keep,
a silent sea.
Let it not weep,
let it just be.

The boat still glides.
The dream still hides.
If it must stay
buried... *okay.*

The Sea and The Rocks
(A story in reverse)

The Silence Before the Storm

Beneath the moon, where waters gleam,
Where waves compose a silver dream,
He sat with shadows by the sea;
Where love once bloomed, now ceased to be.

A gentle breeze, her hair did toss,
Each strand a thread, now at a loss.
He watched, and longed to brush her cheek,
But silence bound what hearts can't speak.

She turned to him with aching grace,
Still searching for that long-lost face.
"What brought us here?" her whisper low,
As tides performed their ebb and flow.

But he just watched the waters break,
On rocks that stood for longing's sake.

They held the sea, they held its roar
But couldn't hold her anymore.

Of Smoke and Sparks (Fifteen Months Ago)

Fifteen moons and one shy sun,
Back when their tale had just begun.
The day was thick with heat and dust,
And time moved slow, as all time must.

He leaned against a weathered wall,
A breath of silence through it all.
A cigarette, half-lit, in his hand;
A flame he tried to understand.

The smoke curled upward like a sigh,
As dreams once buried passed him by.
His mind a maze, his soul a bruise,
A moment's peace was what he'd choose.

And then she came- like winds from shore,
With eyes that knew what life was for.
She didn't shout or raise alarm,
She stopped him with a kind disarm.

"Do you know," she softly said,

"That smoke could kill the song in head?
That sometimes breath, like love, is thin;
And pain begins where smoke gets in?"

He laughed, not cruel, but torn and tired,
His world too worn, his hope expired.
"You think your words will cleanse this place?
That laws can soothe a heart's disgrace?"

She didn't flinch, nor turned away,
She met his pain, and chose to stay.
"Maybe not," she said, "but still,
I'd rather try than leave at will."

The silence hummed like cello strings,
Two strangers bound by broken things.
She walked away, but left her trace,
A ghostly warmth, a sacred grace.

He crushed the butt, half-burnt, half-said,
And watched the ashes paint the red
Of setting sun upon the street;
And knew he'd just begun to meet.

Of Rocks and Waves (Back in the Present)

“Do you know why those rocks exist?”
He asked as breeze and salt both kissed.
“To tame the sea,” he softly said,
Where tides still struck, though love had fled.

She rolled her eyes, her temper flared,
While steamrollers behind them blared.
“Spare me your stupid analogies!”

But he was lost in sea’s retreat,
The splash, the pull, the water’s beat.
It came, it crashed, then turned away;
Yet always came again to stay.

A promise in each foamy throw,
That love, like tide, would ebb then grow.
Yet what are waves when rocks give in?
What is restraint when hearts wear thin?

Of First Confessions (Twelve Months Ago)

Twelve months past in softer light,
A night where stars outshone the night.
She said, “I carry weight and fear,
And I might push if you come near.”

But he, with fire in his gaze,
Said, “Let me walk through all your maze.
I’ll never clip your wings or chain;
Just walk beside you come storm come rain.”

“You with your baggage, I with mine,
Let’s stitch our wounds with borrowed time.
I can’t promise stars or rings,
But can promise you my everything.”

She wept, she smiled, she asked him “Why?”
He said, “I breathe you when I sigh.
You are the pulse beneath my skin,
The war I lose, yet long to win.”

The Cracks Beneath Calm Waters (Nine Months Ago)

Nine months hence, a storm broke through,
A drunken night, an ex’s view.
He questioned trust with trembling voice,
And she defended love’s free choice.

“You knew me wild, you knew me fierce!
Don’t make your fear my freedom’s pierce.”
He tried to speak, to show his dread,
But found his hurting mocked instead.

She spoke with ice, he answered flame,
And neither left the fight the same.
She said, "Don't make me leave you, dear."
He smiled... his mask, his souvenir.

He smiled, though pain had clawed his chest,
Like glass beneath a silken vest.
His love was fierce, his voice was kind;
But hers was storm he could not bind.

The Slips Between the Moments (Four Months Ago)

Four months ago, suspicion crept,
As silence bloomed where trust once slept.
"Who is she?" her tone was tight.
"She's just a friend," he said that night.

But time spent speaks in louder tongues,
Than vows or poems ever sung.
"You choose her eyes, you share her shade,
While mine, you leave to slowly fade."

They fought, they parted, words still raw,
As coldness gripped what once was thaw.
He watched her leave with heavy eyes,

And tasted rain that fell from skies.

A chill, a numbness, soaked his soul,
A voice that once had made him whole;
Now ghosted past his fading frame,
Where even tears forgot his name.

Trainwreck (Two Weeks Ago)

Two weeks past, he saw her there,
With wistful lips and wind-swept hair.
The train was loud, the world a blur,
But all he saw, and heard, was her.

"I don't know where we're going," she sighed.
"I told him go, but then he tried...
To stay with me, to be my light.
But I... I need some space. That is my plight."

Her voice a tremble, like a chord,
Not quite struck, but deeply stored.
She didn't know he heard her ache,
That his heart, too, began to break.

"I think I want to let this go,"
She said, her voice now soft and slow.

The train did halt, the voice called loud;
But he was just a face in crowd.

Letting Go (Present Day)

"I don't feel happy anymore,"
He lied; the waves still kissed the shore.
She begged, "Then speak, let's find a way!"
He turned, but had no words to say.

"It's not about desire or fear,
It's just that love can disappear."
She cried, "You lie! I see your face!
Your voice still holds my warm embrace."

He smiled. "Then let's not dwell or fight,
Let's keep our love in softer light.
Not as a flame that scorched our breath,
But as a ghost that slept through death."

She whispered, "Was this ever real?"
He said, "As real as waves can feel.
But love's a tide; we held, we fell,
We danced, we broke, we wished it well."

The Sea is Free

He rose, his breath a silent cry,
A man who chose to say goodbye.
"I was your rocks," he softly said,
"To still your sea, to calm your dread."

"But now the sea must rage and roam,
It cannot call these rocks its home."
She smirked, "Your metaphors will fade."
He nodded, "So will all we made."

He walked, each footstep laced with rain,
Each step a hymn, each sob a stain.
He didn't turn, though heart did scream;
Of kisses lost and midnight dreams.

And as he left, the sea stayed still,
No storm, no rage, no crashing will.
It missed the rocks it once had fought,
For love, it seemed, is calmly taught.

The sea had changed, its tides had too,
It loved the rocks it once fought through.
It didn't rage, it didn't cry,
It simply watched the stars drift by.

And there it waits, in moonlight's hush;
With every wave, with every gush,
For rocks that walked and won't return,
For love that flickers, never burns.

समंदर और पत्थर की प्रेम कहानी

सन्नाटा और समंदर (वर्तमान)

चाँदनी में लिपटी हुई रात थी,
और समंदर में ख़ास कोई बात थी।
वो चुप था, और वो पास थी,
पर रात ज़रा सी उदास थी।

उसकी ज़ुल्फ़ें हवा में उलझ रही थीं,
जैसे यादें पुराने ख्वाब कह रही थीं।
वो चाहता था छू ले चेहरा उसका,
मगर बस चुप रह गया- बिन कोई धड़कन, बिन धुआँ।

वो देखती रही, ढूंढती रही,
कहाँ गया वो शख़्स जिसे चाहा था कभी?
"ये वाक़ई आख़िरी लम्हा है?" वो पूछ बैठी
मगर जवाब में, वो बस समंदर की लहरें गिनता रहा।

अकस्मात ही पहली मुलाक़ात (पंद्रह महीने पहले)

पंद्रह चाँद पहले की बात है,
जब दो रूहें अजनबी थीं, मगर साथ थीं।
वो थका हुआ, एक दीवार से लगा,
सिगरेट की तपन में सुकून तलाशता रहा।
धुआँ लहराता था जैसे कोई आह,
टूटे हुए लम्हों की थी वो स्याह।

और तब आई वो- भीड़ के खामोशियों में,
जैसे कोई नज़्म उतरी हो धीमी बारिशों में।
"क्या तुम जानते हो, ये धुआँ क्या करता है?"
उसकी आवाज़ में इल्ज़ाम नहीं, परवाह थी।
"कभी-कभी साँस भी इक मोहब्बत होती है,
और धुएँ में घुट के वो भी खोती है।"

वो मुस्कुराया- थका, मगर तल्ख़ नहीं,
उसने कहा, "इस वीराने में यही मेरी तन्हाई सही।"
वो बोली, "शायद नहीं बदल सकूँ ये ज़मीन,
पर कोशिश करने में क्या कमी है?"

वो चली गई, मगर पीछे कुछ छोड़ गई,
वो बात नहीं थी- एक एहसास था, जो दिल छू गई।
उसने सिगरेट बुझाई, और देखा सूरज डूबता
और उस पल को याद किया, जब मोहब्बत ने पहली बार दस्तक दी।

पत्थर और लहरें (वर्तमान)

“जानती हो ये पत्थर क्यों रखे गए यहाँ?”
उसने कहा, समंदर की तरफ़ देखे बिन।
“ताकि समंदर को क़ैद किया जा सके,
ताकि उसकी मौजें शहर न बहा सकें।”

वो चिढ़ सी गई, “फिर से तुम्हारे उलझे हुए मिसालें!”
मगर वो अब भी लहरों में डूबा था;
हर लहर आती, टकराती, फिर लौट जाती।
मगर एक वादा छोड़ जाती- फिर लौटने का।

“इश्क़ भी इन लहरों सा है शायद,”
उसने कहा, “हर बार लौट आता है,
चाहे जितनी चोट मिले,
बस इंतज़ार में रहता है- एक और टकराव का।”

पहली कबूलियत (बारह महीने पहले)

बारह महीने पहले, जब रातें गहरी थीं,
और तारे उनकी आँखों में बसी लकीरें थे।
वो बोली, “मैं आज़ाद हूँ, और रहना चाहती हूँ,
मेरे साथ बोझ है, जो तुम नहीं सह पाओगे।”

वो बोला, “मैं तुम्हारे पंख नहीं बनूँगा,
मगर उड़ने में तुम्हारी मदद ज़रूर करूँगा।”
“मैं तुम्हारे साथ चलूँगा, बिना रोक-टोक के,
बस साथ, एक साया बनकर, सच्चे वक़्त के।”

वो पिघली, मगर डर अभी भी बाकी था,
“तुम इतना क्यूँ चाहते हो मुझे?” उसने पूछा।
वो बोला, “गर पता होता, तो बयान कर देता;
क्यूँकि इश्क़ किया नहीं जाता, बस हो जाता है।”

दरारें, डर और जज़्बात (नौ महीने पहले)

नौ महीने पहले, कोई तूफ़ान था,
प्यार की जगह, शक का उफ़ान था।
एक रात, कुछ दोस्त, थोड़ी शराब,
और एक पुराना रिश्ता; सब एक साथ।

“क्या ग़लत है इसमें?” वो बोली, “मैं आज़ाद हूँ।”
वो बोला, “मैं डरा हुआ हूँ... और तुम्हें खोने से घबराता हूँ।”
वो बोली, “डर और मोहब्बत साथ नहीं चलते,
अगर तुम्हें रोकना है, तो कह दो- मैं रुक जाऊँ।”

उसने कुछ नहीं कहा, बस मुस्कुरा दिया
एक मुस्कान, जो शीशे की तरह चुभती थी।

दूरियाँ और सन्नाटा (चार महीने पहले)

चार महीने पहले, सब कुछ चुप था।
अब न गिले, न शिकवे... बस दूरी थी।

"उस लड़की और तुम में क्या है?" वो पूछ बैठी।
"कुछ नहीं," वो बोला, "बस दोस्ती है।"
"जिस दोस्त संग तुम ज़्यादा वक़्त बिताते हो,
और मुझसे कम..." वो बोली।

वो कुछ समझाना चाहता था,
मगर शब्दों की ज़रूरत अब नहीं बची थी।
वो उठी, और चल पड़ी।
वो बस देखता रहा,
जैसे हर क़दम पे उसका दिल कुछ गिरता रहा।
उसकी आँखें गीली थीं,
मगर वो अब भी कुछ कह नहीं सका।

रेलगाड़ी (दो हफ़्ते पहले)

दो हफ़्ते पहले, लोकल ट्रेन में,
वो दिखी; ख़ामोश, खिड़की से बाहर देखती हुई।

वो पास गया, उसे चौंकाना चाहा
मगर उसकी आवाज़ ने उसे रोक दिया।

वो कह रही थी- "मैंने उसे खुद से दूर भेजा,
ताकि मुझे कुछ वक़्त मिल सके, सोचने का।"
उसकी आवाज़ में झिझक थी, उसकी साँसें भारी।
"शायद मुझे सब ख़त्म कर देना चाहिए..."

ट्रेन रुकी, मगर उसके लिए तो सब कुछ थम सा गया।
वो वहीं था, मगर अब सिर्फ़ एक परछाईं बनकर।

आख़िरी लम्हा (वर्तमान)

"अब मैं खुश नहीं हूँ," उसने कहा,
लहरें अब भी चुपचाप किनारों से मिल रही थीं।

वो गिड़गिड़ाई- "मत जाओ। बात करो..."
मगर उसके लब ख़ामोश थे, सिर्फ़ आँसू बहे।

"हम टूट गए हैं," उसने कहा, "बस इतनी सी बात है।"

"पर हम चाहें तो फिर से जुड़ सकते हैं..." वो बोली।

उसने कहा, "कभी-कभी चाहत भी काफी नहीं होती।"

"हमारे पास क्या बचा है?" उसने पूछा।

"यादें," उसने कहा, "कुछ मीठी, कुछ कड़वी- बस यादें।"

"और समंदर को अब इन पत्थरों की ज़रूरत नहीं..."

समंदर की आज़ादी

वो उठा, और दूर चल पड़ा,
जैसे हर क़दम पर एक वादा टूटा।
उसने पीछे नहीं देखा,
मगर हर आँसू उसकी पीठ पर गिरा।

वो चाहता था दौड़कर गले लग जाए,
मगर दिल बोला, "अब नहीं, अब बस जाने दे।"
वो पत्थर था- जो अब टूटकर कंकड़ बन चुका था।

और समंदर?
वो अब शांत थी- ना बवंडर, ना हलचल।
उसने उस पत्थर से मोहब्बत की थी,
जो उसे थामता था, समझता था।

अब वो आज़ाद थी,
मगर उस आज़ादी में सन्नाटा था।
वो बस देखती रही, इंतज़ार करती रही,
शायद कभी वो पत्थर लौट आए...

क्योंकि मोहब्बत तो वही थी-
जो लौटने का वादा करती है,
फिर चाहे लहरें सौ बार टूटें...

सर्फ़िरा सा एक अफ़साना लिखते हैं चलो

सर्फ़िरा सा एक अफ़साना लिखते हैं चलो,
जहाँ हर लफ़्ज़ साँस ले, हर ख़ामोशी बोले,
जहाँ यादें मुस्कुराएं और सन्नाटे भी रो लें।

चलो एक पल चुरा लें वक़्त की मुट्ठी से,
जहाँ तुम भी अधूरे हो, और मैं भी पूरा नहीं।

चलो कोई नाम ना दें इस रिश्ते को,
बस महसूस करें
जैसे बारिश में भीगती हो कोई दुआ।

ना शुरुआत हो, ना ख़त्म होने की फिक्र,
बस ठहरे रहें
उस एक नज़्म की तरह
जो हर बार नई लगे, फिर भी जानी-पहचानी हो।

सर्फ़िरा सा एक अफ़साना लिखते हैं चलो,
ना काग़ज़ ना क़लम, बस लफ़्ज़ों से,
लफ़्ज़ जो बयां ना करे कोई,

फिर भी कहीं जैसे अंग-अंग में समा जाए...
जैसे कि तुम में मैं बस जाऊं;
और मुझ में कहीं तुम पनाह ले लो।

A Mad Little Fable

Let's write a mad little fable,
Not bound by ink, nor thought too stable.
A tale that sleeps in breath and bone,
That speaks in hush, that weeps alone.

Let silence drip from candlelight,
Let shadows echo soft delight.
We'll steal from time a fleeting thread,
Where love still lingers, left unsaid.

No start, no end, no tale too neat,
Just heartbeats stumbling incomplete...
A whisper lost in rain's soft hum,
A prayer that falls but won't succumb.

Let's write a mad little fable,
With no paper, no pen, just unsaid words;
Words that say nothing, yet somehow remain,
Like blood in the pulse, like warmth in the vein...

Like I melt into you;
And you find shelter somewhere within me.

The Thorn By Her Side

I live beneath her velvet shade,
A spear of silence, darkly made.
She wakes each dawn in ruby grace,
The morning light upon her face.

With every dew that kissed her cheek,
My heart grew sharp, my voice grew weak.
She never knew the words I kept;
The ache I bore, the nights I wept.

For I, a thorn with pointed pride,
Stood watchful always at her side.
And when a hand reached out to steal,
I pricked it raw; I made them feel.

Not out of spite, but out of fear,
That love might take what I held near.
They saw her charm, her perfumed skin;
But none would touch, for I stood in.

I called it care, I named it love,
A curse disguised as guardian glove.
Yet never once did she complain,
Nor question why I bred them pain.

She bloomed despite me- brighter still,
A flame untouched upon the hill.
And I, too proud, too blind to see,
That love must not be tyranny.

But days grew short, and skies turned pale,
Her crimson waned, her petals frail.
No hand came close, no heart took part;
She withered, guarded from the start.

And when she fell, I stayed alone,
A bitter blade, a stem of stone.
No one returned to mourn or know,
For nothing thrives where thorns still grow.

They left the bush, forgot the soil,
No sun, no care, no toiler's toil.
I watched the roots give up their breath,
And felt within; a second death.

I shed my pride, became a leaf,
A scrap of brown, a sign of grief.

And let the wind bear me away,
To places where the soft things lay.

The man returned to claim the past,
His hand now free, his longing vast.
He crushed me under careless shoe;
No thorn, no fight, just morning dew.

But if there's bloom beyond the dirt,
Where souls return from earthly hurt,
Then let me be her petal there,
A fragment soft, beyond compare.

So when they come to pluck her grace,
They'll carry me in her embrace.
And no one need be hurt, or torn;
A rose complete, without a thorn.

काँटा

वो एक गुलाब सी ख़ुशबू, मैं चुभन इक काँटे का,
वो मुस्कान हर सुबह की,
मैं पहरा सूनी रातों का।

हर ओस पर भी मैं नोक बनता,
जो हर पल उसे बचाती थी,
वो खिलती थी धूप में जाकर,
मैं छाँवों में सिसकियाँ छुपाता था।

हाल-ए-दिल बयान न किया,
सीने में दफ़न थे जज़्बात,
जो आया निकट, सो उसको
चुभ गया यूँ अकस्मात।

ईर्ष्या नहीं, प्रेम था,
या शायद था इक डर,
कि कोई तोड़कर ले न जाए
मेरे गुलाब को,
फिर भटकूं मैं आवारा दर-बदर।

चूँकि उसके हर कण पर
हक़ था मेरा; या लगता था यूँ,
वो मुस्कुरा कर कुछ न कहती,
और इस ख़ामोशी को रज़ामंदी मान लिया मैंने।

वो खिलती रही मेरे साये में,
जैसे लौ हो काँच के पीछे,
मैं सोचता रहा; यही तो प्यार है...
पर मैं बेवक़ूफ़, ये जान कर भी समझा नहीं;
बेचारी महफ़ूज़ नहीं... क़ैद थी।

मौसम बदले, रंग भी ढले,
उसकी पंखुड़ियाँ भारी सी हुईं,
कोई पास न आया अबकी बार,
क्योंकि काँटों की हदें चुभने लगीं।

और जब वो झुकी, मुरझाई,
मैं वहीं था, मगर क्या मेरा था?
न कोई रोया, न कोई ठहरा,
जहाँ काँटे हों, वहाँ कौन आए भला?

ज़मीन भी अब रूठी सी थी,
न धूप रही, न बारिश आई,
जड़ें खुद दम तोड़ गईं चुपचाप,
और मैं भी बस मिट्टी में समाया।

गुरूर बिखर कर चकनाचूर हुआ,

और वही हाथ जिनको
कभी काँटा बन चुभता था मैं,
आज उसी ने पैरों तले कुचल दिया।

न दर्द रहा, न पहचान,
ना प्यार, ना गुमान।

अब बस इतनी सी आशा है,
कि इस बार जो खिलूँ फिर से,
तो ऐ बनानेवाले!
मुझे उसकी पंखुड़ी बनाना,
ताकि गर कोई उसे तोड़ने को आए,
तो उसकी आग़ोश में मुझे भी ले जाए।
बन जाऊँ मैं भी गुलाब सी ख़ुशबू,
और ना रहे मुझ में चुभन काँटे का।

The Rose That Bloomed

I bloomed because he didn't know
What sunlight meant to things that grow.
He only saw the bees and hands
The reach of strangers in these lands.

He thought the world would tear me down,
Would pluck me bare, would steal my crown.
But crowns aren't made from fear and thorn
They're shaped in dusk, in light reborn.

He never asked what silence meant
When winds would pause where I was bent.
He mistook my breathless smile
As bond, as vow, as shared exile.

I bloomed despite him- through his shade,
Though roots beneath me had decayed.
Each morning stretched me toward the blue,
While he stood guard; but never grew.
He named it love; that constant bruise,

That sting he swore he'd gladly choose.

He bled for me with sharpened pride,
But never once stood by my side.
He circled me with pain and rule,
And still, I bloomed- the silent fool.
I bore the petals time would waste,
But never tasted summer's taste.

He kept them out, yes; all but one:
The fading light, the setting sun.
And in that dusk, I learned at last;
That beauty dies when held too fast.

I whispered often to the air,
"Let someone come, and just *be* there."
Not to pluck, nor guard, nor grieve,
But simply watch; and let me be.

And when my stem began to bend,
When bloom gave way to bitter end,
He stayed; not soft, but stone, and still,
Afraid to lose what never will.

But I was gone, long long before
My petals touched the garden floor.
My roots had pulled away from ground;

Deaf to it, he never heard the sound.

But silence is a haunting song,
And I had been quiet far too long.
Not broken... just unheard, unseen,
A flower ghost in thorns between.

And if he dreams of me tonight,
Let memory burn, but not hold tight.
Not what he lost, but what he missed:
A fleeting bloom he never kissed.

I never needed blades or bars;
Just rain, just wind, just whispered stars.
And love, not as a war to win;
But instead a place to gently begin.

So next I bloom, let me be thorn;
And find some rose, untouched, unborn.
I'll guard her not with wounds or pride;
But stand beside her, arms untried.

To show her love as he showed pain,
And never let her wilt in vain.
To teach the blade what bloom could mean;
And be the shield I'd never seen.

गुलाब

मैं खिली क्योंकि उसे पता नहीं था
कि धूप क्या करती है फूलों के साथ।
वो बस उन हाथों से डरता रहा,
जो तोड़ ले जाना चाहते थे मुझे, बिन कोई बात।

उसे लगता था कोई छीन ले जाएगा,
मेरी खुशबू, मेरी पहचान।
इसलिए उसने खुद को काँटा बनाया,
और मुझे समझा अपनी जान।

कभी नहीं पूछा मेरी ख़ामोशी क्या कहती है,
यहाँ तो हवा भी मेरे हाल पे तरसती है,
और बारिश भी मद्धम सी बरसती है...

मेरी धुंधली मुस्कान और बेइंतिहा ख़ामोशी;
मानो हो गई उसके लिए रज़ामंदी इस बात की।

मैं उसके साए में नहीं,
उसकी सज़ा के बीच खिली।
हर सुबह मैं सूरज की ओर झुकी,

और वो वहीं; बस काँटा बना रहा,
ना बदली कभी उसकी सोच की गहराई।
वो कहता रहा -यही है प्यार,
ज़रा तरस भी आया था एक बार।

वो ज़ख़्म देता लोगों को मेरे नाम पर,
और चलता रहा झूठ को सच मान कर।
वो नियमों के नाम पर तीलियां बनाता,
मैं फिर भी खामोशी से मुस्कुराई।
पंखुड़ियों में वक़्त बीतता गया,
पर मैंने कभी गर्मियों की नमी ना पाई।

उसने सबको दूर रखा
पर खुद को कभी पास ना लाया।
ढलती धूप में मैंने जाना,
क्या है प्यार, और क्या क़ैद का साया।

मैं जा चुकी थी,
उस पल से काफ़ी पहले जब मेरी पंखुड़ियाँ गिरीं।
मेरी जड़ें खुद ही पीछे हट चुकी थीं,
वो बस ख़ामोश था...
और ख़ामोशी स्वयं एक अकेली गीत होती है।

मैं टूटी नहीं, पर मुरझा ज़रूर गई,
इस क़ैद के दरमियान,
अधूरी मेरी आरज़ू रही।

अगर आज भी वो मुझे याद करता हो,
तो उस ख़ुशबू को याद करे जो वो कभी छू नहीं पाया।
न कि वो जो उसने खोया,
बल्कि उसे जिसे वो कभी महसूस ना कर पाया।

मुझे कभी पहरे की ज़रूरत नहीं थी,
न सुरक्षा की, न वादों की।

बस थोड़ी सी हवा, ज़रा सी धूप,
और अँधेरा आसमान जिसमें हो तारों का रूप।

अब अगर फिर से जनम लूँ मैं,
तो ये चाह है की काँटा बनूँ,
किसी गुलाब की हिफ़ाज़त नहीं;
पर उसके आलिंगन में खिलूँ।

बस इतना अगर जता सकूँ,
के प्यार ना रोकता है, ना टोकता है,
केवल साथ देता है।

अर्सों से

अर्सों से;
दबाया है,
झुकाया है,
जब मन चाहा,
हक जताया है।

रुलाया है,
जलाया है,
अपनों को भी;
दफनाया है।

ना जाने और कितने,
सबने जो ज़ुल्म ढाया है।

चिल्लाओ तो निराशा ,
चुप्पी में दिलासा,
हर बार की वो भाषा;

"ये फितरत है,
ये किस्मत है,

इसी में अपनी बरकत है।"

ये कैसी किस्मत है?

ये किसकी फितरत है?

क्या भूल गया इंसान,
करनी दूसरे की खिदमत है?

क्यूं ज़ुल्म से इंसान,
अब हो रहा सहमत है?

For Ages Now

For ages now!
Been crushed,
Been hushed,
Used like dirt,
Claimed like trust.

Been wept out,
Been burnt down,
Even the loved ones
Put in the ground.

How many more?
This flood of pain
Should they endure?

You scream? They sigh.
You silence? They lie.
Their same old lullaby-

"It's nature's way,

it's fate," they say,
"Your blessings bloom
In this decay."

What kind of fate is this?

Whose kind calls this bliss?

Have we forgotten
We were born to love, not hate?

Why now,
why now suddenly,
we bow down
so easily to tyranny?

And call it worship,
When its blasphemy?

The Sock That Belonged To The Chappal

The master unboxed her, soft and new
A single sock in cream and blue
Still stitched with tags, a satin thread
She smelled of jasmine, not of tread.

A thing of grace, of dainty skin
No mud had touched her toe or shin
She dreamed of heels, of polished floors
Not dusty feet or open doors.

She lived where silks and linens sleep
Where shadows hum and closets weep
Among the lace, the ties, the whites
She never saw the outside nights

But then one dusk, when curtains fell
And hush replaced the dinner bell
She rolled too far, past stitched confines
And met a world beyond her lines.

Beneath the bed, behind the chair
She saw him waiting, standing there
A chappal, cracked, with open seams
With faded red and rubber dreams.

His buckle bent, his tongue half-torn
He looked like he was never worn
By those who dined in marble halls
He lingered near the servant walls.

He bowed his sole. She turned to hide
But something stirred deep down inside
A thread pulled taut, a throb, a heat
The kind one feels but can't repeat

She should have fled. She should have curled
Back to her crisp, untouched world...
But she stayed. She watched. She knew the shame
Still, her ribbing sang his broken name.

A sock of silk. A slipper, worn
The world said pairing them was torn
But hearts don't ask, and threads don't lie
They only stitch what tongues deny

And though the master never knew

Each night she crept to where he did lie;
A stolen glance. A silent sigh
A life unwashed, but warm and shy

At night they met in corners tight
Where moonlight softened even fright
No speech, no vows, no polished names
Just cotton hearts and rubber frames.

She'd press her toe against his skin
He'd close his cracks to draw her in
They didn't fit, not quite, not right;
But still, they tangled every night.

He spoke in creaks, she breathed in threads
They stitched their love beneath the beds
No chandelier had seen such grace
Two castaways in woven lace.

But morning came, it always would
And love must bow, as love oft should
The master woke. The ritual spun
A day begun. A truth undone...

He'd open drawers, reach down with pride
And draw her from the silken side

Her seams would dance in quiet thrill
But joy, she knew, was never still.

For though she hoped, he'd place her near
The one who waited, always there
Instead, she faced a colder fate
The shoe arrived. Precise. Sedate.

He stood in gloss, in black and gold
With silence stitched in leather bold
His laces straight, his arch held high
No mark of mud, no need to try.

He did not bow, he did not see
He only wore what pleased the knee
She slipped inside, too tight, too sore
A prisoner dressed in dress galore.

The chappal watched from under wood
He knew too well. He understood.
He'd learned by now to hide his pain
To see her leave, and not complain

Yet still, each dusk, when day grew old
She'd slide away from leather's hold;
Back to the floor, back to his side
Where nothing ruled, and none could chide.

It happened on a summer noon
When sunlight struck the drawing room
She'd stayed too long beneath the bed
A thread of hers had softly bled.

A speck of dust, a stain too small
A wrinkle in the linen's fall
But mothers see what love will hide
And rules arrive with sharpened pride!

They held her up, they held their breath
A stain, they said, as good as death
This cannot be! This must not stay
The father frowned. The maids looked away

The chappal lay in trembling hush
Then came the broom, the sweep, the brush
They found him there, his rubber torn
His soul too loud for their salon

Throw it out! They said, it smells of skin
Of roads and sweat and villages thin
She was not made for filthy feet
She's been crafted fine for shoes elite!

And so they came, with cloth and foam
They washed her skin, they stitched her home
They soaked her white in scents of rose
As if perfume could cleanse her soul!

The chappal saw, but made no sound
His breath had sunk into the ground
They picked him up, as trash, as old
His years now worth a plastic hold.

Some say he went to servants' care
Some say he vanished in the air
She did not know. She wasn't told
She only wept in folds of gold.

Then came the box, so wide, so deep
A coffin where silks may sleep
And next to her, so proud and tall
The shoe was placed to end it all.

The pair looked perfect, sharp, refined
The match approved by caste and kind
He didn't speak, but clicked his pride
She didn't flinch. She'd learned to hide.

The thread he wore was lined in fame
But could not hold her secret name

She thought of nights on dusty floors
Of chappal laughs and quiet snores.

Now locked in gloss, beneath a bow
She played the role. She smiled just so
But somewhere deep, where fibers part
She tore a little in her heart.

She wore the shoe. She played the part
But slowly came the fall, the start
Of seams unthreading, ribbing torn
Of being used, but never worn

Each day began the same, the same
The hand, the shoe, the absent name
No voice, no heat, no joy, no thrill
Just leather cold, and time to kill

She missed the way the chappal sighed
How dust would cling, how nights would hide
How silence once had meant a kiss
Now silence only meant dismiss.

The shoe walked on, he did not see
The slow unravelling of the sock;
She whispered low inside her heel

Wherever you are, I still feel.

She tore one morning
Not loud,
just soft,
like something tired
of holding on

A thread gave way
along her side,
too faint to hear,
too small to hide.

The master frowned,
his fingers turned
She felt the cold
of being spurned

No ceremony,
no goodbye
Just tossed
as cloth
no longer dry.

She passed the gates,
beyond the glass
Past gardens trimmed

and polished brass.

To where the broken things are thrown
With rusted tin
and bone on bone.

She lay in piles
of frayed regrets
Among the scraps
the world forgets...

And there-
beneath an oil-stained sheet
A chappal stirred
in aching heat.

His buckle torn,
his color dim
But still,
she reached
and curled to him.

He did not ask,
she did not speak
Their silence made
their corners meet.

No one looked
No voices came
No caste,
no rules,
no master's name.

Just broken things
the world forgot
Yet somehow still,
they hurt a lot.

But they lay in peace,
in dirt and grace
A nameless dump,
their meeting place
Where no one cares
what must belong
And love, at last,
is not a wrong.

एक मोज़ा रेशमी, एक चप्पल पुराना

किसी ने डिब्बा खोला धीरे,
और भीतर रेशमी सी
एक मोज़ा- नई, सीधी साधी,
चमक चकाचौंध; ख़ुशबू मोगरे सी।
ना मिट्टी के निशाँ, ना कोई दाग,
ना टूटी सिलाई, ना कोई भाग।
सपनों में बस काँच के फ़र्श,
जहाँ रुकती नहीं कोई गुज़रश।

सिलवटों में बसी थी शराफ़त,
अलमारी में तहज़ीब की राहत।
हर धागा कहता था ये बात,
"मैं सिर्फ़ चलूँगी ऊँची सौगात।"

पर एक शाम, परदे थक चले,
चाँदनी ने जब खिड़की से झाँका
वो लुड़क गई नीचे चुपचाप,
और दिखा उसे एक चप्पल- *बेताब।*

फटी सी पट्टी, गीला-सा तन,
कहीं पे गड्ढा, कहीं पे जतन।
छुपा बैठा था कोने की छाँव में,
जैसे हो शर्म की पनाह में।

उसने मुँह मोड़ा, झुकी निगाह,
पर मोज़े ने देख ली हर आह।
एक धागा खिंचा, एक धड़कन भागी,
जैसे पहली बार रूह हो जागी।

वो रुक सकती थी, लौट भी जाती,
पर आँखें अब पीछे कैसे आतीं?
ना वो शुद्ध थी, ना वो अपवित्र,
बस एक कोना था- मोगरे सा इत्र।

न ऊँच-नीच, न कोई जोड़ी,
बस धड़कनें- छुपी, थोड़ी-थोड़ी।
और मालिक को कुछ भी न पता चला,
हर रात जो चलता उनका फलसफ़ा।
छुप-छुप कर एक चुप्पी से प्यार,
ना माँगा कुछ, ना कोई इज़हार।
एक मोज़ा रेशमी, एक चप्पल पुराना,
फिर भी दोनों में कुछ था दीवाना।

हर रात का था इक वादा ज़रूर,

छत के नीचे, बिस्तर के पास।
ना नाम, ना रस्म, ना कोई रूप,
बस धागों में सिमटी छाँव की धूप।
वो छूती थी उसकी पपड़ी-सी चमड़ी,
वो ओढ़ता उसकी रेशमी ग़र्मी।
दो अधूरे, दो जुदा जहाँ से,
मिलते थे बस, रात की पनाह में।

कभी क़िताबों के नीचे मुलाक़ात,
कभी पर्दों की छाँव में बात।
उसने कहा, "क्यूँ रुकते हो अब भी?"
वो हँसा- थकी, पुरानी हँसी।
"तू चलेगी सुबह किसी और राह,
चाहे जो हो मेरी आरज़ू, मेरी चाह।"
"पर जो रात को मिलता है सुकून,
वो नसीब नहीं बल्कि आलीशान जुनून।"

और फिर, सुबह आ जाती थी सख़्ती से,
अलमारी खुलती, वो थम जाती थी।
मालिक हाथ बढ़ाता, उठाता प्यार से,
पर पहनता उसे - उन जूतों के जोड़े के संग।

चमचमाता, अकड़ा, महँगा सा जूता
न उसे कोई उफ़, न कोई सवाल,
बस पहनना, चलना- यही उसका हाल।
वो चुपचाप सहती हर रोज़ की ये सज़ा,
चप्पल देखता, पर करता ना गिला।

वो खुद में टूटता, खुद में झुकता,
बस हर सुबह अपनी नज़रें चुराता।

पर रातें अब भी उनकी थीं,
जहाँ धूल सिराहना बन था चुका।
वो फिर से मिलते, धागे-सोल में सिमटे,
उलझे बिना बोले, चुपचाप बुनते।
जूता वहीं था, ऊँचाई में सोया,
उसने कभी ना देखा, ना कुछ खोया।
ना जान सका वो मोज़े का दिल,
ना समझ सका उसका इश्क़ मुश्किल।

एक दोपहर, धूप थी तेज़,
काँच की फर्श पर जैसे लावा बरसा,
वो ज़्यादा रुक गई थी इस बार,
एक धागा गिरा- और हो गया वार।

मालकिन की नज़र पड़ी एक दाग़ पर,
"ये क्या है?" वो चिल्लाई घबराकर।
"मिट्टी? निशान? रगड़ का कोई असर?"
अब न बाँकी रही कोई क़सर।

पकड़ के ऊँचा किया गया उसे,
जैसे हो जिरह किसी जुर्म पे खुले में।
"ये क्या हाल बना लिया है इसका?
बिगाड़ दिया इस घर की मर्यादा का हिस्सा।"

चप्पल को ढूँढा झाड़ू ने तेज़,
काँपते कोने में वो मिला आख़िर,
तंग, गुमसुम, चुप-सा पड़ा था,
जैसे बस अपने हिस्से की सज़ा के लिए खड़ा था।

"इससे बदबू है, गली की छाप है,
मोज़े का चप्पल संग होना पाप है!"
कहा गया, "फेंक दो इसे कहीं दूर,
ये हमारे मोज़े की न बन सके नूर।"

मोज़े को फिर से धुलवाया गया,
गुलाब के पानी में गलवाया गया।
दाग़ जो था, वो मिट तो गया,
पर जो बचा, वो था एक साया सा नया।

चप्पल को शायद नौकरों को दे दिया,
या कूड़े में फेंक, नाम भी ले लिया।
मोज़े को किसी ने बताया नहीं,
बस उसकी रातें चुप हो गईं कहीं।

फिर आई एक बंधन सुनहरी,
रेशमी रिबन, चुप्पी की पहरी।
बगल में था वो जूता, वही उँचा,
जिसे पहनकर कुछ न महसूस होता था।

"जोड़ी बनी," बोले सब ख़ुश होकर,

“क़ाबिल है ये, एक जैसे होकर।
इनकी जोड़ी कितनी आलीशान है।
जूता और मोज़ा साथ हों, यही तो विधान है!”

वो ना बोला, वो ना हँसी,
दोनों में बस चुप्पी बसी।
वो जूते का रुतबा था, वो घर की लाज,
पर किसी ने ना पढ़ी उसकी भीतरी साज़।
वो सोचती रही... धूल भरे पल,
वो कोने की साँझ, वो छुपा हुआ कल।

अब हर रंग में थी बस एक परछाईं,
हर रेशे में दर्द की सच्चाई।
उसकी मुस्कान अब लिपटी थी झूठ से,
और दिल का धागा टूटता गया कहीं;
एक तमन्ना थी मन में,
जो धीरे धीरे छूटता गया कहीं।

कहने को अब जोड़ी बनी थी,
मालिक की पसंद, रस्में सजी थीं।
हर सुबह वही क्रम, वही हाल,
जूते के संग- मगर दिल बेहाल।

रेशों में अब कुछ बचा ना था,
हर पहनावा एक फ़र्ज़ सा था।

वो जूता- चमचमाता, पर मौन,
ना समझ, ना स्पर्श, ना कोई कौन।
वो उसे ओढ़ता जैसे ताज,
ना देखे उसकी थकी आवाज़।

ना कोई स्पर्श, ना अपनापन,
बस दिन गुज़रे- व्यर्थ जीवन।
अब हर दिन था रेशों का घाव,
ना कोई सुकून, ना कोई ठांव।
जूता चलता, ऊँचा सिर लिये,
और वो- हर मोड़ पर गुमसुम सिये।

धीरे-धीरे रंग भी ढल गई,
सुगंध भी अब फीकी सी पढ़ गई।
धागे ढीले, आत्मा थकी,
हर सुबह, एक साँस रुकी।
कभी रात को बुदबुदाई धीमे,
"तू जहाँ भी है, बस वहीं हूँ मैं जी में।"
जूता ना सुनता, ना समझता कुछ,
बस चलता रहता- अपना रुख़।

एक सुबह यूँ ही...
चुपचाप फट गई वो
ना चीख़, ना चुभन,
बस जैसे कोई थक गया हो
सदियों की आदत से।

धागा उधड़ा, किनारा टूटा,
किसी ने ध्यान भी ना दिया।

मालिक ने आँखें मोड़ी,
कहा- "अब बेकार है ये,"
और एक पल में
कूड़े की ओर उछाल दिया।

वो उड़ती रही हवाओं में,
दरवाज़ों से बाहर,
सीमाओं से पार,
जहाँ ना थी अलमारी की दीवार,
ना मर्यादा की लकीर।

कूड़े के ढेर में
धूप की जली रोटियाँ,
मिर्ची की छिलकियाँ,
और पुराने मनके पड़े थे।

और वहीं,
एक जानी-पहचानी सी ख़ुशबू;
फटी सी पट्टी,
धूल में सनी एक साँस

वो चप्पल।
वो पास था।

टूटा, पर ठंडा नहीं।
थका, पर भुला नहीं।
उसने कुछ पूछा नहीं।
उसने कुछ कहा नहीं।

वो बस चुपचाप
उसके पास सरक आया।
वो पास गई
धूल की उस ख़ामोशी में
जहाँ ना मालिक था,
ना कोई जोड़ी की परिभाषा।

ना कोई देखा,
ना कोई बोला,
ना जात,
ना नाम,
ना समाज ने रोका।
बस टूटी चीज़ें,
जो ज़माने ने भुला दी थीं
पर फिर भी,
कहीं ना कहीं,
अब भी रोती थीं।

वो मिले
धूल में,
चुप्पी में,

एक अनाम कोने में।
जहाँ कोई ये ना पूछे
कि किसे किसके साथ होना था।
जहाँ मोहब्बत...
आख़िरकार...
ग़लती नहीं थी।

ग़ुफ़्तगू

"फोन पर बात करना अच्छा नहीं लगता..."
"क्यूँ? मिलकर भी बात करें,
तो बातें फिर भी वही रहेंगी ना?"

हाँ... लफ़्ज़ तो वही होंगे,
पर लहज़ा बदल जाएगा,
तेरी साँसों की गर्मी
फ़िज़ा में घुली मिलेगी।

और जब पास होती हो,
मैं शेर नहीं कहता,
बस देखता हूँ तुम्हें
जैसे कोई भूली हुई नज़्म
ख़ुद से मिलने आई हो।

हाँ, हमारे शब्द तो वही होंगे;
पर आँखों के बीच
कोई अलग ही ग़ुफ़्तगू होगी।

Conversation

"I don't like talking on the phone..."
"Why? Even if we met,
wouldn't the words be the same?"

Maybe.

But over the phone,
your voice feels borrowed.
Like it's dressed for someone else.
Not me.

In person,
your breath touches mine.
Even silence
feels like a confession.

When you're near,
I don't reach for metaphors.
I just look at you
like a forgotten poem

finally remembering its ending.

Yes, we might still say the same things...
but between our eyes,
a different kind of truth would speak.

Love & Longing

Love was worship
not something done,
but something *become*.
A slow unfolding of flame
without a name.

Longing was madness
a fever without fire,
a tide that rose
even in drought.

But tell me-
must there be a name
for the ache to be real?
Must someone arrive
for the heart
to have felt?

I have loved
without a face.

I have waited
for echoes.
I lit candles
for shadows
that never grew legs.
Prayed
to silence
as if it could hold me.

Perhaps the hunger
to love
is older
than love itself.
A river
that remembers the sea
but never reaches.

Somewhere in me,
something broke
long before you.
Not from loss
but from being
unfinished.

A thread was pulled,
not by you,
but by the idea

of being *found.*

I am not one.
I never was.
I am pieces
of music,
of wind,
of a soul
that once burned whole.

Scattered now
light through glass,
flame through breath,
atom
searching atom.

To love,
perhaps,
is not to give yourself away
but to return
to the ache
that made you.

To touch not the skin
but the space between
where longing hums
like an unsung hymn.

And if no one ever comes
if the door never knocks,
if no eyes ever hold mine
still,
I have felt the fire.

And maybe
that is enough.
To ache.
To want.
To burn without name,
without end.

To know
that somewhere,
the whole I once was
is still splitting
still searching
for the pieces
I was meant to become.

इश्क़ इबादत है, और मोहब्बत जुनून

गर इश्क़ इबादत है,
और मोहब्बत है जुनून
तो क्या वजूद ज़रूरी है
उस अग्न को महसूस करने के लिए?

क्या कोई चेहरा होना चाहिए
जिससे दिल लगे?
या सिर्फ़ तड़प
ही काफी होती है
रूह को छूने के लिए?

मैंने चाहा है-
बिन वादा,
बिन मंज़िल,
बेतुकी,
बेहिसाब
वह आभास
जिसे सिर्फ़ दिल समझता है।

मैंने दीए जलाए
उन सायों के लिए
जो कभी ज़मीन पर उतरे नहीं।
मैंने आवाज़ दी
उन ख़ामोशियों को
जो बाँहें बनकर भी
कभी लिपटी नहीं।

शायद ये चाह
किसी को पाने की नहीं
बस खुद से मिलने का प्रयास है,
अपने अंदर के सूनेपन से
होती गुफ्तगू की तरह।

कभी लगता है
हम सब रूहों के टुकड़े हैं
एक ही रोशनी से निकले,
अब अलग-अलग दिशाओं में
अपने बाँकी हिस्सों को ढूंढ़ते हुए।

मैं कोई एक नहीं हूँ,
महज़ अधूरा हूँ,
मगर तपता हूँ
हर रोज़
अपनी ही आग़ोश में।

और शायद

मोहब्बत का मतलब
किसी को पा जाना नहीं,
बल्कि उस प्यास को जीना है
जो कभी बुझती ही नहीं।

छूना ज़रूरी नहीं होता
कभी फ़ासलों में भी
एक अनकहा राग छिपा होता है,
एक अनकही नज़्म,
एक अधूरी कविता।

और शायद
इतना काफ़ी है।

तरसना,
चाहना,
बिना नाम के,
बिना अंजाम के
जलते रहना।

क्योंकि
कहीं न कहीं,
वो मुकम्मलपन
जो मैं कभी तलाशता था,
अब भी टूट रहा है
अब भी तलाश में है
उन टुकड़ों की

जो मुझे फिर से मैं बना दें।

और हो जाऊँ मैं, फिर से पूरा,
वो हिस्सा जो भटका अधूरा,
हाड़, मांस, पसली और ख़ून;
जो समझ चुका कि
इश्क़ इबादत है,
और मोहब्बत... जुनून।

She Liked Coffee, I Liked Tea

She liked coffee, I liked tea;
And that was the beginning of our misery.
I should have seen, but I refused to see
What love would make us eventually be.

She moved like wind with secrets to spill,
Laughed in octaves that could bend your will.
We fell in sync like chords in a song,
And swore to each other, we couldn't be wrong.

She was chaos with lipstick and stars in her hair,
I was pages and patterns and calculated care.
She showed me how to dance in the rain,
I taught her that stillness isn't always pain.

We made homes in hotel rooms,
Wrote stories on napkins, chased full moons.
Even our silences had rhythm back then
Whatever I lacked, she somehow knew.

And for a while
We believed.

But then-

She cried in the shower, hidden from view.
I timed it with the fan. Pretended I never knew.

She'd speak, I'd scroll.
She'd reach, I'd fold.

The laughter was gone.
Warmth- *gone.*

You okay?
I'm fine.
Just tired.
Same.

Space.
Silence.
Stiffness.

She packed.
I watched.

Keys on table.
Door.
Shut.

Stillness.
Breath.
Gone.

We were a spark in the wrong season.
A song in the wrong key.
She liked coffee, I liked tea
And that was to be our tragedy.

उसे कॉफ़ी पसंद थी, मुझे चाय

उसे कॉफ़ी पसंद थी, मुझे चाय
इस रिश्ते का बस इतना था अभिप्राय।
समझना चाहिए था, पर था मैं नासमझ
की ये प्यार की मंजिल कुछ और ही है।

वो चलती थी जैसे राज़ हो हवाओं में
और हँसती थी जैसे सरगम हो दुआओं में
हम मिले थे किसी गीत की तरह
जिसे लिखा गया हो सिर्फ हमारे लिए, बेपरवाह

वो थी बादलों में बिजली सी,
मैं था शांत से धूप में कोई दिया
उसने सिखाया बारिश में नाचना
मैंने सिखाया उसे ख़ामोशी में जीना

होटल के कमरे भी घर लगने लगे
नैपकिनों पर कहानियाँ बुनने लगे
हमारी ख़ामोशियाँ भी बोलती थीं
और जो मुझमें नहीं था, वो उसमें था, वो जानती थी

और कुछ वक़्त के लिए
हमने यक़ीन किया

पर फिर-

वो रोती थी शॉवर के नीचे, चुप-चाप
मैं चलाता था पंखा, जैसे कुछ सुना ही न हो

वो बोलती थी, मैं फ़ोन में खो जाता
वो हाथ बढ़ाती, मैं दूर हो जाता

हँसी ग़ायब सी हो गई,
प्यार भी धीरे धीरे ओझल हुआ

ठीक हो?
हाँ।
थक गया हूँ।
मैं भी।

फ़ासला।
चुप्पी।
थकान

वो गई
मैं देखता रहा
चाबियाँ मेज़ पर

दरवाज़ा
बंद

सन्नाटा
साँस
सूनापन

हम एक ग़लत मौसम की चिंगारी थे
ग़लत सुर में लिखा एक गीत

उसे कॉफ़ी पसंद थी, मुझे चाय
बस यही था इस रिश्ते का अभिप्राय।

Bodies Fall, But Souls Do Not

Bodies fall-
but souls do not.
The flesh may break,
but love forgot?
Never.

They say the dead no longer speak,
but listen close-
and you may seek
the whispers left in desert sand
where Laila still holds Majnu's hand.

Or ask Mirza and his bride,
whose silence flows with river's tide.
Their tale may end in mortal breath,
but not in time
and not in death.

Romeo and Juliet died, they say,

but love refused to walk away.
And Savitri, with steady breath,
didn't just fight fate;
she undid death.

We weep when lovers leave this land,
but don't you see?
They now expand
beyond the names we knew them by,
beyond the earth,
beyond the sky.

True love-
it lived before the clock,
before the sun could even talk.
It breathed before the stars were born,
and it shall bloom
past every mourn.

Now free of rules,
of blood and bone,
they float where only love has flown.
No chains, no names,
no cage, no creed;
just soul to soul,
just need to need.

So when you see two lovers part,
don’t clench your chest,
don’t break your heart.
Instead, just light a single flame
and whisper softly
each their name-

"You’re free of time,
of name, of skin.
You are the fire
that burns within.
You are the hush
between each breath;
for souls in love
outlive all death."

लोग बिखरते हैं, रूह नहीं

लोग बिखरते हैं,
रूह नहीं।

जिस्म तो बस इक साया था,
आज है, कल कहीं नहीं।

मगर इश्क़?
इश्क़ तो वो सांस थी
जो वक़्त से पहले चली,
और वक़्त के बाद भी थमेगी नहीं।

लैला से पूछो, मजनूं से जानो,
क्या उनका इश्क़ मिट्टी में सो गया था?
या हर रेत की लकीर में आज भी
वो छाँव बनकर रो गया था?

मिर्ज़ा की ख़ामोशी में,
साहिबा की इक आह है।
उनकी दास्तान अब भी
हर टूटे दिल की राह है।

रोमियो-जूलियट ने जिस्म छोड़े,
पर रूहों का मिलन ना टूटा।
सावित्री ने वक्त को मोड़ा,
मौत का वादा भी झूठा।

जो कहते हैं-
इश्क़ मरता है जिस्म के साथ,
वो क्या जानें
कि रूहें चूमती हैं तारे हर रात।

वो इश्क़ जो वक़्त से पहले था,
वो वक़्त के बाद भी रहेगा सदा।
ना मज़हब की लकीर, ना रिवाज़ की दीवार,
इश्क़ तो उड़ान है... बिना पर, बिना भार।

अब ना कोई रिश्ता, ना कोई नाम,
ना हक़ जताने का पुराना पैग़ाम।
अब वो कुछ और ही हैं
जैसे लहरों में खोया हुआ गीत,
या चाँदनी में छुपा कोई मीत।
ना चिठ्ठियाँ, ना वादे, ना दस्तूर,
बस रूह से रूह तक एक नूर।

तो जब कोई प्रेमी गर दुनिया से जाए,
कृपया करके एक दीप जलाएँ।
और कहें-

"अब तुम हो अमर, अब तुम हो स्वतंत्र,
ना वक़्त का डर, ना मरने का मंत्र।
अब तुम रूह हो, तुम रोशनी हो,
तुम मोहब्बत हो, तुम बंदगी हो।
जिसे सच में चाहा गया हो कहीं,
वो मिटता नहीं... कभी नहीं।"

लोग बिखरते हैं,
रूह नहीं।

The Eyes, The Heart and The Soul

The First Fracture

You came in with silence
folded under your sleeves-
a silence I knew.

"Dad," you whispered,
"I think it's over."

And in your eyes,
I saw the tremble
of a boy who had just learned
that love can leave.

You believe tonight
that the world has ended.

But let me show you
how it often does son;

only to begin again.

The Eyes

She walked past me-
a comet made of skin,
and I,
a starless boy,
let her gravity pull me in.

She didn't know my name,
but oh, the world did whisper hers...
like wind across a chapel,
like secrets stitched across the universe.

Her laughter rang like chimes in May,
her footsteps light as skies in gray.
I fell not deep, but high instead;
on clouds of dreams that love had fed.

My mind made maps around her name,
my eye, enchanted, stoked the flame.
I saw her face and built a life;
of job, of house, of child, of wife.

But one day,

she turned,
and softly said,
“I’m in love with someone else instead.”

And just like that,
the dream I’d spun
were threadless...
the morning sun
refused to rise;
I walked in dusk
for months disguised.

That day,
I stopped believing in love.
I swore I'd never trust the sky again-
for what are stars
but lies etched in flame?

The Heart

I was a shell.
No song, no skin,
just a man
in the memory of who he had been.

No compass,

no shore.
Even mirrors did me abhor.

And then, she found me-
not like thunder,
but like tea placed on a windowsill
without a word.

She didn't ask where I had gone;
she only stayed,
asking that I return.

Her eyes
didn't burn,
they warmed.

She laughed like forgiveness,
moved like rain,
held me without question,
kissed me without gain.

She stitched my shattered hours,
sewed sunlight into my name.

She was peace,
she was promise,
she was flame.

And I-
I worshipped her.

She was the altar.
I was the ash.

I called it love
because I needed her.
I needed her like air,
and she gave it
without asking why
I was drowning.

But somewhere between rescue
and rhythm,
between arms
and always-
that ache returned.

Love does not survive
in gratitude's echo.
It needs more than worship.

She deserved more
than the man who loved her
because she made him whole.

And so it ended-
not with storms,
but with the sound
of two people breathing
apart.

The Soul

And then...
when I was done looking,
she appeared-
not dazzling,
not divine.
Almost asinine.

She did not flow like a verse from a ballad,
For she was more a punctuation.

Not the kind
that ends a sentence,
but the kind
that lets it breathe.

She wasn't the sort
I'd have written sonnets for.

But sonnets, I learned,
can also be lived.

My mind did not fall for her.
My heart,
still scarred,
did not stir.

But my soul-
my soul stood up in its sleep
and said,
"There she is."

She did not fix me.
She did not fight for me.
She simply sat beside me
and time forgot to move.

And so did I.

Her love had no conditions.
No reasons.
No rescue.

She was not a lighthouse.
She was the shore
that didn't need to shine

to feel like home.

And one day-
as she walked toward me
on our wedding day,
not like a bride,
but like a quiet answer

I finally understood:
The universe had broken me
only so I could be
the shape that fit hers.

In conclusion

So son,
this ache you wear tonight;
don't hide it.

Let it teach you.

The one who left
was not your end,
but the way your story
learns to bend.

I once loved with my eyes;
for beauty glows.
I once loved with my heart;
where kindness grows.

But the love that stayed,
the one that bloomed,
was the one my soul already knew.

And one day,
without looking,
without rhyme or reason,
someone will arrive
who feels like
a pause in chaos.

You won't chase her.
You won't even know.
But something quiet in your bones
will bow.

And you'll call it love.
Not because you must.
But because
it asks nothing of you
but truth.

प्रेम प्रसंग

तन्हाई की वो शाम

आज तुम चुप थे...
जैसे शाम ने अपने जूते उतार दिए हों
और ज़मीन पर पाँव रख दिया हो।

"पापा...
सब ख़त्म हो गया..."
बस इतना कहा,
पर उस एक वाक्य में
पूरी दुनिया टूटती सुनाई दी।

मैं मुस्कुराया नहीं,
मैं बस ठहर गया...
क्योंकि उस दर्द की धुन
मैं पहले भी सुन चुका हूँ।

तुम सोचते हो कि सब बिखर गया है,
कि अब कुछ भी पहले जैसा नहीं होगा।

पर बेटा,
कुछ कहूँ?
कभी-कभी टूटना ज़रूरी होता है
ताकि एक नया रूप बन सके।

आँखों का पहला प्रेम प्रसंग

वो गुज़री थी जैसे कोहरा हो,
या जैसे धूप का कोई पहरा हो,
हवा की तरह छू के निकली,
बस एक पल का मानो चेहरा हो।

किसी ने कहा बेहद ख़ूबसूरत है वो,
किसी ने कहा वो है शबनम सी,
पर आँखें तो अब भी उनके आँखों पर अटकी थी
जो कहतीं की जन्नत की हूर थी वो।

मैंने तो उसके नाम से ही,
कायनात की दीवारें रंग डाली थीं,
ख़्वाबों का इक घर था बसाया,
और साँसों की परछाइयाँ संग लाया।

हर ख्वाहिश उसी से निकली थी,
हर मोड़ उसी के हिस्से का था,
कौन पढ़ता नज़्में किताबों में,
जब दिल में ज़िंदा एक किस्सा था।

फिर एक दिन अकस्मात ही बोली-
"मैं अब किसी और की हो चली,"

आवाज़ थी धीमी, पर ऐसा लगा
जैसे वक़्त ने साँसें खो दीं

वो पल था जैसे बारिश गिरी हो
किसी नाज़ुक सी काग़ज़ की कश्ती पे,
और मैं बह चला
तूफ़ान में जैसे ढूंढ़त सहारा।

उस दिन मैंने यक़ीन तोड़ दिया,
इश्क़ से, सपनों से, मोहब्बत से ,
और तब से हर रौशनी में
छुपा सा डर बैठा रहा रात से।

जिसे दिल ने चाहा

तब मैं खुद से ख़फा था शायद,
आईना देखता तो डरता था,
ज़िन्दगी एक बंद किताब थी,
जिसे हर कोई पढ़ कर फेंक चुका था।

मोहब्बत पर से ऐतबार उठ चुका था,
हर रिश्ता अधूरा सा लगता था,
जैसे कोई राग अधूरी हो,

या साज़ ख़ामोशी से डरता था।

उसी वक़्त वो आई थी,
ना चाँद सी, ना बारिश सी,
बस जैसे थकी हुई दोपहर में
खिड़की से आती मद्धम सी हवा।

उसने कुछ पूछा नहीं मुझसे,
ना मेरी तन्हाई का हिसाब मांगा,
बस चुपचाप मेरे पास बैठ गई,
और हर टूटे लम्हे को गले लगा लिया।

वो मेरा मरहम भी बनी,
और मेरी वजह भी,
मैं टूटा हुआ तारा था,
वो मेरी पूरी गगन भी।

वो हँसती तो लगता था,
जैसे सदीयों से रुकी साँसें चल पड़ी हों,
वो छूती थी तो लगता था,
जैसे पत्थर में भी नमी सी पल पड़ी हो।

मैंने उसे चाहा,
जैसे कोई भूखा रोटी से प्यार करे,
या जैसे कोई डूबता हुआ
किनारे को ख़ुदा समझे।

पर शायद...
इश्क़, शुक्रगुज़ारी का मोहताज नहीं होता,
जिसे बचाने की आदत हो,
वो कब तक मोहब्बत निभाता?

धीरे-धीरे हम दोनों
अलग लहरों में बहने लगे,
ना लड़ाई, ना शिकवा...
बस सांसें थमने लगीं, पल कटने लगे।

और तब जाना-
वो मसीहा थी मेरी टूटी दुनिया की,
मगर मसीहाओं से मोहब्बत नहीं होती,
सिर्फ एक एहसान बाकी रह जाता है।

जिसका इंतज़ार रूह को था

ना रंग था उसमें नया,
ना कोई अलग सी बात थी,
वो बाकी सब जैसी थी शायद,
फिर भी उसमें कुछ ख़ास थी।

ना नज़रें ठहरती थीं उसपे,
ना दिल धड़कता था बेवजह,
पर जब भी पास बैठती थी,
तो लगता था...

जैसे शोर थम गया हो कहीं।

ना उसने मुझसे कुछ माँगा,
ना मैंने कुछ खोया,
बस वो साथ रही
जैसे छाँव किसी पेड़ की
न दिखती, न कहती,
पर हर दुपहरी साथ वो रहती।

मैं ना उससे मोहब्बत करना चाहता था,
ना करने से बचता था,
बस धीरे-धीरे
मेरे अंदर कुछ पिघलता रहा।

ना दिमाग ने हाँ कहा था,
ना दिल ने इज़हार किया,
पर मेरी रूह...
मेरी रूह चुपचाप मुस्कुरा उठी थी।

वो ना मेरा इलाज बनी,
ना मेरा इनाम,
बस मेरी आदत बन गई-
जैसे हर सुबह की चाय,
या शाम की खिड़की।

शादी वाले दिन,
जब वो मेरी ओर चली

ना लिबास भारी था,
ना मेकअप की चमक...
फिर भी ऐसा लगा
जैसे जवाब चलकर मेरी ओर आ रहा हो।

और तब समझ में आया-
जो टूटा था पहले,
वो सब टूटना ज़रूरी था
ताकि मैं उस रूप में ढल सकूँ
जो उसकी रूह को पहचान सके।

आख़िरकार

तो हाँ बेटा,
आज जो तू रोया है
वो तेरी उम्र का सबसे सच्चा आँसू था शायद।
पर ये आख़िरी नहीं है...
ये तो पहली बारिश है

जिसे तू आज "आख़िरी" कह रहा है,
वो शायद तेरा पहला पन्ना हो।

तू बोले-
"अब और मोहब्बत नहीं होगी।"
मैं भी कभी यही बोला था।
कसमें खाई थीं,

किताबें जलाई थीं,
पर मोहब्बत...
वो तो बिना दस्तक चले आती है।

मैंने एक को देखा,
तो आँखों ने प्यार किया
क्योंकि चेहरा ख़ूबसूरत था।

फिर एक आई,
जिसका दिल दरिया था,
तो दिल बह गया।

पर जो साथ रह गई,
उसमें कुछ भी 'ख़ास' नहीं था...
सिवाय इस बात के कि
मेरी रूह ने उसे देखा,
पहचाना,
और कहा के बस;
"यही है।"

प्यार न आँखें चुनती हैं,
न दिल समझ पाता है,
प्यार...
शायद वही होता है
जहाँ सुकून साँस लेने लगे
और वक़्त बैठ जाए
तेरे पास, तेरी तरह।

एक दिन,
जब तू ढूँढना भी छोड़ देगा,

कोई आएगी-
ना फ़रिश्ता, ना परी,
महज़ एक इंसान।

और तेरा दिल नहीं,
तेरी रूह बोलेगी-
"मैं इससे पहले भी मिला हूँ कहीं।"

The Boy Who Knew The Stars

I used to gaze at the stars every night,
And they used to gaze right back at me;
Like quiet friends with blinking eyes,
Perched beyond the mango tree.

The fields were wide, the winds were slow,
The roads were dust, the ponds were deep.
The dogs would chase the evening glow,
And hush would rock the house to sleep.

Barefoot dreams on summer ground,
Swinging high on bamboo poles,
Fireflies danced without a sound,
And kites would rise like rescued souls.

Each night I'd sit in the porch's hush,
The village wrapped in lullaby;
And through the cracks of roof and rush,
The stars would answer from the sky.

But time is cruel- it walks, it burns.
It gives you dreams, then never returns.
It tears the child out from your chest,
And leaves the ache, but not the rest.

The city rewires the way you pray.
It sells your silence, names it grey.
You learn to smile through silent scars,
While concrete buries all you are.

I rise, I run, I chase the same
Dead-end trains that never came.
The sky's a rumour, rarely seen.
The stars? Refused. Replaced. *Routine.*

I write of roots I can't recall,
Of things I don't really know anymore;
I sell iterations of what they want,
And bury the truth I knew before.

Each night I try to look above-
But haze and glass have blurred the fight.
The stars were outbid long ago
By cars, by windows, by city light.
And now the sky no longer glows;

But flickers like a tired show.

Some nights, I swear- I close my eyes
And hear my laughter in disguise.
But then the sirens start to scream,
And I forget that I can dream.

But one day, when the noise has thinned,
And I've grown tired of chasing wind;
I'll pack no pride, no grand success,
Just silence wrapped in brokenness.

I will return... not to reclaim,
But just to find the boy I named.
The one who stared with quiet eyes,
At stars that lit up country skies.

I'll walk the path, not to be seen,
But to remember where I've been.
And sit once more where night runs deep,
And let the fields and shadows sleep.

And maybe then, beneath that dome,
I'll feel a light I used to know
The stars will blink... then disappear slow,
And I'll know they saw me, even so.

तारे जिसके अज़ीज़ थे

हर रात मैं बैठकर तारे गिनता,
और वो मेरे लिए गिनती रखते थे
जैसे खामोश चमकती आँखें
किसी भूले दोस्त से मिलते थे।

खेत थे फैले, सुस्त थी हवा,
तालाब थे गहरे- थमे, हरे।
कुत्ते भागते सूरज की पूँछ पकड़े,
और रातें मानो माशूक़ के चेहरे।

जब बाक़ी सब नींद में होते,
मैं अकेला बरामदे में जा बैठता
हवा सिरहाने कोई बात रखती,
और तारे... मुझसे बातें करती।

मगर वक़्त बेरहम है
चलता है, जलता है,
पर लौटता नहीं।
जो बच्चा सीने में धड़कता था,

उसे छीन लिया एकदम से
अब वहाँ कुछ भी नहीं।

शहर दुआओं की तर्ज़ बदलता है,
चुप्पियों को नाम देता है- "ख़ता"।
मुस्कान पहननी पड़ती है यहाँ,
जब कंक्रीट हर पल तुम्हें दफ़्न है करता।

उठता हूँ, दौड़ता हूँ, वही दिन, वही रात
उन ट्रेनों के पीछे जो कभी न आईं।
आसमान अब अफ़वाह बन चुका है,
तारे? अब बस नींद में देते दिखाई।

जिन जड़ों से कभी जुड़ा था मैं,
अब वो यादें भी किराए की लगती हैं।
जो वो सुनना चाहते हैं, वो झूठ मैं बेच आता हूँ,
और अपना सच कहीं रोज़ गाढ़ आता हूँ, गहराई में।

हर रात ऊपर देखने की कोशिश करता हूँ मैं,
पर आसमान अब वैसा रहा ही कहाँ है।
तारे जैसे हार गए हों इस खेल में,
अब सिर्फ़ धुएँ और शीशे का जहाँ है।

हाँ, टिमटिमाहट अब भी बाकी है रात में,
पर वो है गाड़ियों की, सड़कों की रौशनी।
उन खिड़कियों की, जहाँ सपने अब भी जागते हैं,
जो तारे कभी खुद सपने हुआ करते थे,

अब उनकी जगह अधूरे ख्वाबों ने ले ली है।

कभी-कभी पलकें भीग जाती हैं यूँ ही,
और किसी बीते हँसी की परछाईं उतर आती है।
लेकिन तभी सायरन चीरता है सन्नाटा,
और वो सपना... फिर खो जाता है।

पर एक दिन, जब शोर थम जाएगा,
और ये दौड़ थक जाएगी मुझसे
ना जीत लेकर, ना कोई तमग़ा,
सिर्फ़ टूटी हुई चुप्पी साथ लाऊँगा मैं।

लौटूँगा; कामयाबी लिए नहीं,
बस उस बच्चे को ढूँढने,
जो कभी चुपचाप आसमान को देखता था,
और तारे... जो उसे पहचानते थे।

चलूँगा उसी पगडंडी पर, चुपचाप,
जहाँ मेरी परछाई भी मुझसे बातें करे।
बैठूँगा उसी पुराने कोने में,
जहाँ मिट्टी की ख़ुशबू अब भी ठहरी हो शायद।

मैं फिर बैठ कर वहाँ तारे गिनूँगा...
और वो फिर शायद मेरे लिए गिनती रखेंगे।

तू इस रूह की फ़रियाद बन गई

तू इस रूह की फ़रियाद बन गई,
मोहब्बत बनते-बनते बस याद बन गई।

जिस हँसी से तन्हाई होती थी दूर,
अब उसी तन्हाई की सौग़ात बन गई।

कुछ धूप पड़ी थी मेरे बरामदे में तेरी,
वो दीवारों पे ठहरी इक बात बन गई।

तेरे होंठों की नमी अब भी कप पर है,
वो नमी तेरी आख़िरी निशाँ बन गई।

इक चम्मच चाय में तू घुलती थी रोज़,
मेरे प्याले की आख़िरी मिठास बन गई।

वो उधड़ी रज़ाई, जिसमें लिपटे थे कभी,
अब सर्द हवाओं की इक याद बन गई।

जिस गिटार के तार बुना करती थी तू,
तू उसी की बिखरी साज़ बन गई।

हर दिन माँगा था दुआ की तरह,
वही दुआ अब मेरी ख़ैरात बन गई।

तू इस रूह की फ़रियाद बन गई,
मोहब्बत बनते-बनते...
बस याद बन गई।

The Cry My Soul Never Spoke

You became the cry
my soul never spoke,
you were meant to be love
but became its smoke.

The laugh that once
sent solitude away
now makes a home in me,
and asks to forever stay.

Your sunlight pooled
along my porch at noon,
then fixed on quiet walls
each and every afternoon.

The coffee mug still keeps
the moisture your lips left,
that tender trace within,
the last of you I've kept.

You used to melt
like sugar in my tea,
my cup's last sweetness,
left there just for me.

That fraying quilt
we argued under, stayed,
and now lets the winter in
to corners where memory lay.

Your guitar by the window,
night on night,
now hums in loosened strings,
a broken light.

I asked for you each day,
the way one prays,
still pining, still holding
to old days' haze.

You were meant to be love,
but became its smoke.
You became the cry
my soul never spoke.

जनाज़ा

एक इल्तिज़ा है तुझसे, ऐ मौत,
कि आएगा जब मिलने को तू,
वादा है, हँसते हँसते साथ चलूँगा।

बस तू भी इतना सा वादा कर,
कि जनाज़ा मेरा
उसी खिड़की तले गुज़रे...
जहाँ बरसों पहले
मैं रहता था खड़ा।

उसकी ताक में,

यूँ फ़िराक़ में,

इश्क़ की राख में...

बस इतनी-सी तमन्ना कर दे पूरी,
जिस दीदार को
ज़िंदगी भर तरसी ये रूह,
मौत पे वो मुकम्मल हो जाए।

Coffin

I have a small request, Death.
When you come for me,
I promise,
I will walk with you smiling.

Only-
Let them carry my coffin
beneath the window
where I stood for years,
a wick at noon,
a moth at night.

At her pane,

in my pain,

in love's ash
like winter rain.

Grant me that one mercy.

What my soul starved
for all its life,
complete in death;
let it arrive.

One last look,
a faint memory within
my soul's respite.

लफ़्ज़

लफ़्ज़ बड़े बेईमान हैं,
जो कहना चाहता हूँ, कह नहीं पाता हूँ।
अर्थ को जब पकड़ने जाऊँ,
अपने ही अंदर कहीं खो सा जाता हूँ।

जैसे होंठों पर आधी पंक्ति
रुककर साँस की डोरी तोड़े;
स्याही बरसात समझकर कागज़
हर सच की नमी को पूरा सोखे।

जो जज़्बात आँखों में रहती तुम्हारी,
ज़ुबान पर आते ही जाती हैं उलझ,
पलकें अनुवाद करती हैं सब कुछ,
लफ़्ज़ बनते ही वो जाते हैं बिखर।

रोज़ नए लफ़्ज़ बटोर हम लाते,
भाषा की बाज़ार से मोल-तोल कर,
पर फिर भी बड़े बेईमान और ज़ालिम हैं ये,
जब ज़रूरत हो, तब चले जाते दामन छोड़कर।

काश ख़याल सीधे आते हमें समझ,
फिर मतलब की ज़रूरत ना होती,
इक नज़र में बयाँ करते सब कुछ,
ख़ामोशी ही सबकी ज़ुबान होती।

लफ़्ज़ बड़े बेईमान हैं,
जो कहना चाहता हूँ, कह नहीं पाता हूँ,
पर आँखों में तेरे सच छुपा है,
आजकल उन्हीं में कहीं खो सा जाता हूँ।

Words

Words are unfaithful,
What I ache to confess goes unsaid.
I reach for meaning,
Yet lose myself instead;
A child in tall grass
Calling his name to the wind, unheard.

On my lips, a half-line falters,
The thread of breath is torn.
Ink falls down like rain,
And the page drinks truth, yet thirsts again.

The real feelings live in your eyes...
Deep, surreal, no disguise.
But when I try to speak what I see,
They collapse, leaving nothing of me.

Words are unfaithful.
Your eyes translate everything,
But the moment sound is born, it scatters.

We polish our words,
Weigh them, barter their shine,
Bring them home from the market of language
And still they betray,
Slipping like coins through my grasp
When silence is what I need most.

Words are unfaithful.

Perhaps speech is a ladder
To a roof we never reach.
Perhaps thought arrives whole,
And language fractures it into shards.

Yet your eyes hold the sky unbroken,
And in their depth I glimpse a truth
No tongue could ever teach.

If only meaning came as it is
A glance carrying the river entire,
No oars, No effort,
Only stillness to ferry us through.
Silence would be our shared tongue,
Salt-lit, simple, *sure.*

Words are unfaithful.

What I would tell you drifts unsaid.
The truth curls in your eyes,
A small animal unafraid of the dark.
I go there now to find it,
and lose myself, again,
On purpose.

ख़्वाब

रोज़ ख़्वाबों में आती हो,
यूँ रूह में समाती हो;
पर पलकें जो खोलूँ मैं,
क्यों ओझल हो जाती हो?

अधूरी रात बन कर तुम,
सुबह की धूप में ढल जाती हो।
खुशबू बनकर दस्तक देती हो,
फिर धुंध बन ग़ायब हो जाती हो।

रोज़ यूँ ख़्वाबों में आती हो,
दिल के दरमियाँ बस तुम जाती हो;
पलकें मूँद कर जीता हूँ आजकल,
क्योंकि खोलते ही ओझल हो जाती हो।

Where Shadows Meet

Each night you return, a breath of flame,
Yet morning denies that you ever came.
You lie in the hollows where silence weeps,
Then rise with the dawn, uncalled by name.

You are the night unfinished, torn;
A half-spoken verse that mocks the morn.
You arrive as fragrance; tender, near,
Yet vanish as mist before it's born.

My heart is a house with an open door,
Each echo inside repeats you more.
I live with my eyelids closed and still,
For when they open, you are no more.

And I wonder if yearning is all we keep,
A dream rehearsed, but never complete.
For love survives not in touch, but ache,
In the hollow of absence, where shadows meet.

www.ingramcontent.com/pod-product-compliance
Lightning Source LLC
Chambersburg PA
CBHW050526240926
51846CB00003B/715
9789373141817